The Orders of Ministry in The United Methodist Church

The Orders of Ministry in The United Methodist Church

John E. Harnish

Foreword by Thomas E. Frank

ABINGDON PRESS

Nashville

THE ORDERS OF MINISTRY IN THE UNITED METHODIST CHURCH

This book is printed on recycled, acid-free paper.

Library of Congress Cataloging-in-Publication Data

Harnish, John E., 1947–
    The orders of ministry in the United Methodist Church / by John E. Harnish.
      p. cm.
    Includes bibliographical references (p.) and index.
    ISBN 0-687-09216-7 (alk. paper)
      1. United Methodist Church (U.S.)—Clergy. 2. Ordination—United Methodist Church (U.S.) I. Title.

BX8345 .H27 2000
262'.1476—dc21

                                       00-058299

Scripture quotations are from the New Revised Standard Version Bible, copyright © 1989, by the Division of Christian Education of the National Council of the Churches of Christ in the United States of America.

Quotations from *The Book of Discipline of The United Methodist Church—1996* © 1996 by The United Methodist Publishing House and from *Services for the Ordering of Ministry in The United Methodist Church* (Provisional Texts), copyright © 1998 The United Methodist Publishing House. Used by permission.

Quotations from *Polity, Practice and Mission of The United Methodist Church* by Thomas E. Frank © 1997 by Abingdon Press used by permission.

Quotations from *Baptism, Eucharist and Ministry* © World Council of Churches, Publications, P.O. Box 2100, CH-1211 Geneva 2. Used with permission.

Quotations from David Tripp, "Ordination, Laying on of Hands, and the Role of the Laity," *Doxology* (December 1998), Akron, Ohio, are used by permission.

Quotations from Bishop William Cannon, "Meaning of Ministry in Methodism," *Methodist History* 8, no. 1 (October 1969); and Jeffrey P. Mickle, "A Comparison of the Doctrine of Ministry in Francis Asbury and Philip Otterbein," *Methodist History* 19, no. 4 (July 1981) are used by permission.

Quotations from personal letter and report to the United Methodist Ordinal Task Force by Robin W. Lovin are used by permission.

Quotations from "Bishops' Statement on Laying on of Hands" are used by permission.

00 01 02 03 04 05 06 07 08 09—10 9 8 7 6 5 4 3 2 1

MANUFACTURED IN THE UNITED STATES OF AMERICA

CONTENTS

Appendixes

FOREWORD

Thomas E. Frank

Contemporary United Methodism is living its way into a new ordering of ministry marked by both promise and confusion. As Jack Harnish shows so effectively in these pages, this manner of understanding ministry by living our way into it—practically, functionally, with operational definitions and situational flexibility—has typified American churches of Wesleyan and Methodist heritage throughout their histories. The 1996 General Conference, however, introduced forms and rationales for ordained ministry and conference membership that radically break with long-standing traditions. Now, as if the church has paused to catch its breath, neither the 1996 nor the 2000 General Conference has authorized a commission to develop further proposals for change in the ministry. This is a time for sorting out new dynamics, settling into new forms, and reflecting on the problems and possibilities before us.

Thus Jack Harnish's book comes at exactly the right time. Who better to guide the reader through the complex issues and emerging questions of ordained ministry than one who has been immersed in them as pastor, teacher, and executive charged with interpreting and guiding the implementation of the *Discipline?* This book is an indispensable resource for boards of ordained ministry. It provides critical education for candidates for ordained ministry. It will be helpful and provocative for both lay and ordained church leaders and particularly useful for delegates to future General Conferences.

Right from the beginning, this text focuses the reader's attention on a range of issues crucial to working out an understanding of ordained ministry in United Methodism. Harnish shows us the strengths and weaknesses of the current theological grounding for ordained ministry in the church, walks us through the new services for commissioning and ordination, draws us into definitions and functions of the orders of deacon and elder, examines the role of local pastors, and all along the way will not let us avoid the hard questions of how American Wesleyan pragmatism meshes with ecclesiological traditions. He pushes us to ask in what ways United Methodism can continue to be an effective ecumenical partner in the search for convergence among traditions of ordained ministry.

Harnish's book is timely, then, for reasons that transcend current practical issues being worked out in every annual conference and in many local churches. For much of the last century, and particularly in the last forty years, the church's attention has been focused on a broader understanding of ministry grounded in baptism and expressed through the witness and service of the whole people of God. This has provided a theological basis for the ministry of laypeople in ways never articulated so clearly or compellingly.

Having established the grounding of that common ministry, however, the church must also turn its attention more deliberately to articulating how ordained ministry is understood both theologically and functionally within the community of faith. As Harnish shows, United Methodism and its predecessor denominations have never provided much rationale for ordination in the *Discipline*. It has not been unusual, for example, for a General Conference to add a term like "Order" to the definition of an elder in the church with no paragraph defining what "Order" means, or to adopt the contemporary term "servant leadership" without saying how such language is connected with ecclesiological offices. The church has been more concerned with being "clergy dependent," to quote a major report to the 2000 General Conference, than with defining the clergy offices theologically and ecclesiologically.

Jack Harnish's book comes at the right time to spark a much-needed discussion of ordination. He demonstrates the eclectic roots and practices of United Methodist ordination, explores the complex relationship of ordination and conference membership, and asks critical questions about how the orders of deacon and elder are now to be understood in relation to each other and to the ministry of the laity. He shows that to the extent the orders are more clearly defined, the ministries of the whole people of God are enhanced and empowered. If his book can be a catalyst for helping the church come to a common understanding of ordained ministry, Harnish's evident passion for the church's ministries will have proved a gift to us all.

Thomas E. Frank
Associate Professor of Church Administration
   and Congregational Life
Director of Methodist Studies
Candler School of Theology
Emory University

A Word of Acknowledgment

My first sermon was preached from behind a piano bench with my twin brother standing close beside me. It was directed to Mom, Dad, and our black cocker spaniel. Needless to say, we were very young, preschool probably, and "playing church." I do not remember the text. All I know is that my call and my ministry to this day are deeply rooted in that living room on Grand Avenue and in parents who lived their ministry long before the term "ministry of all Christians" was in vogue. My dad probably should have been a preacher, but he sold auto parts and sent twin boys instead.

Working on this manuscript has reminded me once again of the debt I owe my parents, Sunday school teachers, summer camp counselors, and pastors who nurtured my call and encouraged me on the way. Reverend W. R. Ross, a retired pastor in my home church, whose grandsons, named Heitzenrater, have made their own mark on ordained ministry, took my brother and me under his wing and sent us off in faith, believing that the Lord could use us.

In this project I have also been surrounded by a host of colleagues who have kept me honest by offering their critical comments and wise counsel, particularly Jimmy Carr, Russell Richey, Thomas Frank, Robin Lovin, and Bishop David Lawson. Mary Hodge, my assistant, has spent countless hours making sense of my manuscript and my pencil-scratches.

I offer a word of profound thanks to the General Board of Higher Education and Ministry and to Dr. Roger Ireson, General Secretary, for a board policy that encourages study leaves; to Duke Divinity School for supporting my independent study through the Duke Fellows program; and to the Louisville Institute for a study grant for religious leaders, which made possible my research and writing.

To all these, and most of all to John Wesley, I am forever grateful for the calling and privilege of traveling the connection as an itinerant Methodist preacher! After seven creative and challenging years with the Board of Higher Education and Ministry, I have returned to my first calling: to preach God's Word and love God's people in the local church. In the words of Francis Asbury, "Live or die, I must ride!"

INTRODUCTION

Ministry in the Methodist tradition is perhaps as difficult a subject to delineate with precision and confidence as any in the entire area of ecclesiology. The reason for this is that ministry in Methodist history has been defined almost entirely by circumstance. Practical necessity in this instance has dictated theology as well as determined polity and devised the strategy for mission. The ministry as much as any other element or entity in Methodism is the result of improvisation. It has always been functional and pragmatic.

—Bishop William Cannon, *Methodist History*

Background

After more than twenty years of ministry studies, the 1996 General Conference of The United Methodist Church approved a new ordering that includes some of the most significant changes in our polity since the original pattern for ordination was instituted in the Christmas Conference in 1784. In reality, we had

13

been involved in ministry study dealing with a variety of topics for fifty-two years, dating back to 1944. Richard Heitzenrater gives an insightful and concise history of ministry studies from 1944 through 1988.[1]

As Bishop Cannon noted, one consistent factor is the Methodist emphasis on the "functional and pragmatic."[2] In terms of mission, this has been one of our strengths: Polity and church order are driven by a desire to communicate the gospel effectively. In a sense, the Methodist approach to church life is to ask first, "What works?" and then to reflect on the theological implications. This approach has governed the evolution of Methodist ministry and characterized the various ministry studies over the years. Most ministry studies tended to focus on the specific roles and functions of persons in ministry rather than on the larger questions of the meaning and purpose of ordination. In fact, as Franz Hildebrandt lamented in 1960, "There is not very much official material on the Methodist doctrine of ordination; there is no theological definition in the *Discipline*."[3]

One can question whether the *Book of Discipline* is the appropriate place for a "theological definition," but thirty-six years and ten general conferences later, Hildebrandt's basic assessment still holds true. Except for Dennis Campbell's book *Yoke of Obedience,* little has been written regarding United Methodist ordination and the theology surrounding it. In the first edition of Campbell's book, published in 1988, he skillfully summarizes the development of ministry in the Wesleyan tradition up to that time. The soon-to-be-published second edition will interpret the new ordering of ministry and will be a significant resource for the whole Church.

In one of the first analytical articles to be written since the 1996 General Conference, "The Theology of Ordained Ministry in The United Methodist Church," William Lawrence comes to this conclusion:

> *Polity,* manifest in ecclesiastical actions that grant authorizations for ministry, *is an expression of theology.* The real problem facing United Methodists is not trying to describe who is authorized to do

what. Rather, the real problem is to understand the whole situation theologically.[4]

The 1996 legislation will shape the identity and practice of the Church for the foreseeable future, but the General Conference by its very nature is a legislative body and is not organized for theological reflection. Though the proposal that came from the Council of Bishops was based on serious theological reflection, the conference was, quite naturally, more concerned about "who is authorized to do what" than it was to "understand the whole situation theologically." After one quadrennium the Church is only beginning to comprehend the changes brought about by the General Conference of 1996. Many of the ecumenical ramifications of the new ordering of ministry are yet to unfold. As has often been the case in Methodism's pragmatic and functional approach, we have worked out the practice first and are now thinking through the theological implications.

The Church needs time and opportunity for serious wrestling with the theological and ecclesiastical dimensions of our new ordering of ministry. To that end, in 1999 the Division of Ordained Ministry called for a series of consultations during the 2001–2004 quadrennium to discuss our emerging theology of ordination and ministry in an arena of theological reflection away from the legislative pressure of a General Conference. It is to be hoped that these consultations will result in a new definition of ordination that will incorporate the changes made in 1996 and in an in-depth consideration of our history, practice, and mission.

In relation to the creation of the new Order of Deacon in full connection, the action of the 1996 General Conference can be compared with similar changes in the British Methodist Church and in other communions in recent years that have attempted to take seriously the calling of persons in ministries other than the typical presbyter/elder. In this legislation the office of deacon was significantly redefined as a ministry distinct from the ministry of the elder. Rooted in the historic diaconate, it is also quite different from the previous Order of Deacon in The United Methodist Church and is, in fact, a new creation.

Part of the impetus for this rethinking was the *Baptism, Eucharist and Ministry* document of the World Council of Churches, which suggests three Orders—deacon, elder/presbyter, and bishop—but fails to give a clear understanding of the unique ministry of the deacon. Theological and historical reflection will be important not only to our self-understanding as United Methodists, but also for our relationship with our ecumenical colleagues and other branches of the global Methodist family if we are to seek closer ecumenical ties and deeper understanding. This is especially true in the dialogue with our partners in the Consultation on Church Union (COCU; now Church of Christ Uniting) and the Pan-Methodist dialogue.

The changes in ordained ministry that were brought about by the 1996 legislation are likely to be as significant as the mergers of 1939 and 1968. I believe, in fact, that some of the decisions of the 1996 General Conference reflect issues involved in bringing together the Methodist Protestant and Methodist Episcopal churches in 1939 and the merger of the Methodist and Evangelical United Brethren churches in 1968. Tension between our Anglican/Wesleyan/Asburian roots in episcopal polity and the Reformed presbyterial polity of Otterbein, though never acknowledged in the General Conference debate, stands in the background of this shift in our understanding of ministry.

I am basically an itinerant Methodist preacher. I do not presume to have definitive answers to the many questions related to our new ordering of ministry and would not attempt either to speak for the board on which I serve or to resolve these many issues on my own. My experience, however, has involved me in the heat and the heart of these issues. As a delegate to the 1988 and 1992 General Conferences and an elected member of the Board of Higher Education and Ministry from 1988 to 1993, I was involved in various discussions concerning ordained ministry and served as a member of a reflection group within the board that contributed to the dialogue. In 1993 I became the associate general secretary of the Division of Ordained Ministry, and since the 1996 General Conference the staff of the division has been intensely involved in the implementation of the ministry legislation. Out of that experience I have endeavored to learn, question, and dialogue about these issues with a variety of colleagues. This volume represents my learning and my understanding of the history and the issues involved in the new ordering of ministry.

The General Conference in 2000 made relatively few changes in the ordering of ministry adopted in 1996, presenting us with an opportunity that has not existed since 1964—a quadrennium without a committee to study the ministry! As we adapt to our new polity, we need to reflect on its implications historically, theologically, and ecumenically. This book represents my attempt to raise cogent issues, affirm basic principles, and encourage thoughtful reflection among United Methodist theologians, historians, church executives, ordained clergy, and laity in order to assist the Church in shaping and ordering ministry for the effective proclamation of the gospel and the building of the reign of God in society.

Focusing the Issues

I believe the following areas are critical to a proper understanding of our new ordering of ministry:

History and identity: How does the new ordering of ministry maintain fidelity with our tradition(s) and express our identity?

Of specific interest would be John Wesley's understanding of the ordinations for America, Francis Asbury's ordination at the Christmas Conference, Philip William Otterbein's approach to ministry, and the contribution of Jacob Albright. These four men were the primary forces in the origin of what was to become The United Methodist Church. The action of the 1996 conference should be evaluated in light of these roots.

Lay ministry and ordained ministry: What is the relationship of ordained ministry to the ministry of all Christians, and how will we affirm the fullness of ministry?

One of the most significant movements in the Christian church today is a new (or renewed) emphasis on the ministry of all baptized Christians. This takes different forms in different denominations, but throughout the church there is a desire to affirm the ministry of all Christians that grows out of baptism.

In addition to the need for a new understanding of ordination, the new concept of commissioning must be defined in order to distinguish between these two acts. Since commissioning is already used for missionaries and deaconesses, which include laity as well as clergy, what distinguishes the commissioning of ministers from the commissioning of probationers? We will also continue to consecrate bishops. Ordination, commissioning, and consecration: All three concepts need clear definition.

Also significant is the distinction between the ministry of all Christians and the calling and ministry of laypersons serving in specialized ministries as a career. The former office of diaconal minister evolved from the office of certified lay worker as a way of affirming lay professionals and distinguishing their calling. Without that office we must find ways of affirming the importance of laypersons in specialized ministries lest we fall into further clericalization of ministry.

Finally, the new definition of clergy includes not only ordained elders and deacons, but also unordained local pastors and commissioned ministers. How does ordination relate to one's identity as United Methodist clergy?

Apostolic ministry and servant leadership: What is servant leadership, and how will the tradition of apostolic ministry be continued in the new ordering of ministry?

The 1996 *Discipline* replaced the short-lived term "representative ministry" with "servant leadership." However, as Thomas Frank has noted, the term *servant leadership* "is not a phrase particular to ecclesiology," and "the term is not specifically connected with the church's historic manner of ordering its communal life, namely the language of offices."[5] Since the term is used to refer to both ordained and lay leadership in the local church and is not defined, one is left with some confusion as to what it says about ordination.

The historic and ecclesiological term "apostolic ministry" still

18

appears in ¶ 302, but is not used as the primary definition of ordination. Since one of the historic roles of the ordained is to carry on the apostolic tradition, the question of how to affirm this tradition under the new definition becomes important to the self-understanding of United Methodist clergy and to our ecumenical relationships.

Deacon and elder: How will our new ordering of ministry shape our understanding of the identity of the elder and the deacon and the relationship between these two Orders?

From time to time different elements of the various strands that constitute United Methodist tradition seem to gain prominence. I believe that the 1996 ministry legislation is a step away from our Methodist Episcopal (Roman Catholic/Anglican) roots, in favor of an emphasis closer to the Reformed and Protestant strands, as represented by United Brethren and Methodist Protestant traditions, first, by breaking from the tradition of elders' being first ordained deacon; and second, by significantly altering the historic relationship between ordination and sacrament.

The new Order of Deacon in full connection emphasizes the variety of ministries to which a person can be called and expands the ways in which ordination can be used to authorize and send persons in service for the Church. This calls for a new and broader definition of ordination. Though the desire of the General Conference may have been to affirm the distinct role of the deacon and the elder, the resulting demarcation has the potential to create an unhealthy separation between the sacramental and the servant ministries, between the diaconal ministry and the apostolic ministry. How will we address the distinct character of these two ordinations and still maintain a unity in ministry?

Ordination, conference membership, and itinerary: How does our new ordering of ministry affect the relationship between ordination and conference membership, particularly as it relates to itinerary?

Historically, Methodism maintained what Thomas Frank calls the "dual framework—of conference membership and ordination."[6] Frank suggests that the action of the 1996 General Conference "will shake the dual framework to its foundations. For the first time in Methodist history, there is an ordained order of persons who do not itinerate and who initiate their own place of employment."[7] Deacons will be full members of the conference, but will not itinerate. At the same time we are expanding the use of local pastors, who are not guaranteed an appointment. How will the new understanding of ordination relate to itineracy and conference membership?

Ordination and the sacraments: What is the link between ordination and sacramental administration?

We now have an ordained ministry that does not have sacramental authority. At the same time, we have expanded the use of non-ordained local pastors, who are granted authority under the supervision of an elder to celebrate the sacraments in the congregations to which they are appointed. Though previously this was seen as Methodism's missional necessity, now all commissioned ministers preparing for ordination as elders will be licensed as local pastors during probation and will administer the sacraments for three years without ordination. These two changes—ordained clergy without sacramental authority and the broader use of non-ordained clergy with sacramental authority— may be the most significant theological and historical changes brought about by the 1996 legislation.

United Methodist ordination and ecumenism: What are the implications for our relationship with the global Methodist family and our ecumenical partners?

In 1989 British Methodism revised its ministry to provide for the "Methodist Order of Deacon," replacing the discontinued office of deaconess. In several branches of the Methodist family, the lay office of deaconess continues to have an important role in the servant ministry of the Church. The central conferences, which have freedom to adapt the *Book of Discipline*, hold differing views on the new ministry legislation. In the ecumenical community there is consensus on the need for a revitalized diaconate, but significant differences exist as to its relationship to the lay ministry, the sacraments, the elder/presbyter/priest, and other issues of polity. Some denominations have lay elders as well as deacons.

Today United Methodism is seeking closer ties with other Methodist denominations and with our COCU partners; our new Orders, however, were adopted by the General Conference with limited attempts to connect with other traditions. We must be clear about our understanding of ordination if we are both to relate to others with integrity and to learn from them. As we move away from our long-standing tradition and from our similarity to the Roman Catholic/Anglican/Orthodox tradition, we are moving in a new direction.

Ordination and the mission of the Church: Will these new Orders enable us to communicate the gospel more effectively and fulfill the mission of Christ in the world?

Orders and polity are, after all, a means to an end, not an end in themselves. For John Wesley, church order was subservient to the mission to proclaim the gospel. The 1996 General Conference clearly affirmed the mission of the church "to make disciples of Jesus Christ by proclaiming the good news of God's grace and thus seeking the fulfillment of God's reign and realm in the world" (*Book of Discipline,* ¶ 200).[8] Concerning ministry, the *Discipline* says: "Beyond the diverse forms of ministry is this ultimate concern: that all persons will be brought into a saving relationship with God through Jesus Christ and be renewed after the image of their creator" (¶ 105).

The final test of our ordering of ministry will be whether or not it helps the Church fulfill its mission to serve the world for which Christ died: to proclaim the gospel and to make disciples of Jesus Christ. I believe that the tradition and witness of Methodism continue to be valid and effective tools for accomplishing this task. How the action of the 1996 General Conference will assist us in accomplishing that ministry is yet to be seen.

CHAPTER ONE

History and Identity

Have always, therefore, printed in your remembrance, how great a treasure is committed to your charge.
> —*John Wesley's* Sunday Services of the
> Methodists in North America

John Wesley

Sometime after 2:00 AM on September 1, 1784, in a private home in Bristol, England, John Wesley, James Creighton, and Thomas Coke laid their hands on Richard Whatcoat and Thomas Vasey, ordaining them deacons. The following day Wesley ordained them elders, giving them certificates that read in part, "I have this day set apart for the said work, as elder, by the imposition of my hands and prayer . . . to feed the flock of Christ, and to administer Baptism and the Lord's Supper according to the usage of the Church of England." He then laid his hands on Thomas Coke, naming him superintendent, with authority to ordain. Coke's certificate read, "Know all men that I John Wesley think myself to be providentially called at this time to set apart some persons for the work of ministry in America. And therefore under the protection of Almighty God, and with a single eye to his glory, I have this day set aside as a Superintendent, by the imposition of my hands and prayers . . . Thomas Coke."[1] He sent them to America clearly intending that they should do the same for Francis Asbury and other preachers in America, which they did at the Christmas Conference of 1784, when Francis Asbury was first ordained a deacon, then elder, and finally a superintendent or bishop. With that the Methodist Episcopal Church was born, and the original pattern for Methodist ordination was established, a pattern that remained essentially intact for 212 years in the Methodist Episcopal/Methodist/United Methodist Church.[2]

Wesley's extraordinary step, taken by one who continued to espouse loyalty to the order of the Church of England, created much debate, beginning with John's own brother, Charles. When he learned of it, Charles wrote:

> *So easily are Bishops made*
> *By man's or woman's whim?*
> *Wesley his hands on Coke hath laid,*
> *But who laid hands on him?*

Of Asbury's ordination by Thomas Coke, Charles quipped:

> *A Roman emperor, 'tis said,*
> *His favourite horse a consul made;*
> *But Coke brings other things to pass,*
> *He makes a bishop of an ass.*[3]

Beginning with Charles, many have questioned the appropriateness of Wesley's action. As we move into our third century, the conclusion of Raymond George is correct: "That Methodism is now a Church does not depend on the validity of what was done in 1784; . . . we assert that Methodism is a Church, and being a Church, both can and does ordain."[4]

That today we understand ourselves as a church, not as a society, and that as a church we ordain ministers is well established. For our purposes it is not necessary to go into the appropriateness of Wesley's action, but rather to discover those foundational principles at work in Wesley's ordinations that may be important to our identity today.

Methodist preachers and Anglican priests

Linda Durbin says, "There is no clearly stated "theology of ordination" in Wesley, but there is what he did, and his writing."[5] From what he did and what he wrote, it is clear Wesley affirmed the tradition of threefold ordination as practiced in the Anglican Church—that is, ordination at the hands of a bishop, first as deacon, then as priest (or elder or presbyter); and the ordination of the bishop, who then had the authority to ordain. In England Wesley's preachers were to work alongside this regular ordained ministry, not to replace it. He described them as "extraordinary messengers"—that is, out of the ordinary way, designed to "(1) provoke the regular ministers to jealousy; (2) to supply their lack of service toward those who are perishing for want of knowledge."[6] Their ministry was strictly limited to preaching and evangelism. His preachers were not even allowed to baptize children, a privilege that has always been available to any Christian in emergency situations. All sacramental ministries were to be received from ordained priests of the Anglican Church, and all Methodists were expected to participate in the worship life of the local parish church.[7] It was the lack of effective preaching that inspired Wesley to turn loose his "extraordinary messengers" in hopes of renewing the life of the church he so loved.

Wesley set clear limits for their work, which was simply to preach the gospel. "Did we ever appoint you to administer the sacraments; to exercise the priestly office? Such a design never entered into our mind; it was the farthest from our thoughts; and if any preacher had taken such a step we should have looked upon it as a palpable break of this rule and consequently a recantation of our connexion."[8] Though ultimately Wesley would, in fact, ordain persons for ministry in America where the sacramental ministry of the Anglican Church was in disarray because of the revolution, later in Scotland, and eventually for the Methodists in England, in his lifetime he continued to recognize the authority of the ordained ministry of the Church of England.

David Shipley identifies some of the distinguishing elements of Wesley's preachers, whether ordained clergy or lay: (1) They were nicknamed Methodists "because they preached . . . not necessarily by what they preached or how they preached, but *that* they preached" (italics added). This meant that they did not read sermons prepared by others, but focused on the direct proclamation of the *kerygma*, the central message, the core of biblical faith. (2) They recognized their ministry as a response to God's "call to preach" and "the personal presence of the Holy Spirit as the sole source of power." This emphasis on the inward call was not required for ordination in the Church of England and was distinctively Wesleyan.[9] Finally, (3) "a preacher called Methodist was distinguished by an unquenchable sense of urgency manifested in itineracy. It was not the love of travel that kept him on the move. It was, rather, a profound intuition that the life of the church . . . was . . . at stake *in his generation.*"[10] The urgency of a call to preach marked the lives of these early Methodists, and though some of them were ordained Anglican clergy, Wesley did not believe that this preaching ministry required ordination.

Ordinations for America

When the need in America brought him to the point of ordaining persons for that work, Wesley followed the pattern of the Anglican orders, as can be seen from the original ordination certificates and *The Sunday Services for the Methodists in North America,* Wesley's revision of the *Book of Common Prayer,* which he sent with Coke as the basis for the new church in America. Major changes included the abridgment of the Articles of Religion from thirty-nine to twenty-four, but the services of ordination remained essentially intact except for the use of the term "elder" instead of priest and "superintendent" instead of bishop. Methodism was born out of the Roman Catholic/Anglican tradition that included ordination as deacon followed by ordination as elder through an episcopate, and the ordination of the superintendent that would function as the *episcopos* in the new church.

A word needs to be said, of course, about the tension between Wesley's commitment to the episcopal pattern of the Church of

England and his decision to proceed with the ordinations for America even though he was not a properly ordained bishop. As early as 1746 Wesley became convinced, partly through reading Peter King's *An Inquiry Into the Constitution, Discipline, Unity and Worship of the Primitive Church* and Edward Stillingfleet's *Irenicum*, that bishops and presbyters are essentially one order and that under certain circumstances, presbyters have the right to ordain. Wesley writes:

> Lord King's account of the primitive church convinced me, many years ago, that Bishops and Presbyters are of the same order and consequently have the same right to ordain. For many years I have been importuned, from time to time, to exercise this right, by ordaining part of our Traveling Preachers; but I have still refused, not only for peace sake, but because I was determined, as little as possible, to violate the established order of the national Church to which I belonged.[11]

It was only after the bishop of London refused his request to ordain some of the Methodist preachers bound for America, and only after 1783, when the Treaty of Paris ended the Revolutionary War and with it the authority of the bishop of London over America, that Wesley moved in this direction. He concludes that

> . . . the case is far different between England and America. Here there are Bishops who have legal jurisdiction. In America there are none, neither any parish Ministers. So that, for some hundred miles together, there is none either to baptize or to administer the Lord's Supper. Here, therefore, my scruples are at an end; and I conceive myself at full liberty, as I violate no order, and invade no man's right, by appointing and sending labourers into the harvest.[12]

The statistics dramatize the need. Dennis Campbell notes that "in 1784 there were 14,998 Methodists in the United States being served by eighty-three non-ordained, itinerant Methodist preachers."[13] The situation produced nothing short of a leadership crisis in these early days of the movement as well as the desperate need for sacramental ministry. Linda Durbin writes, "Wesley saw himself as a 'missionary episkopos,' a presbyter uniquely required to exercise his inherent right to ordain."[14]

The priority of the mission

Of course, Wesley's commitment to the ordering of ministry in the Anglican tradition must always be balanced with his over-arching concern for the effective proclamation of the gospel and the fulfillment of the mission for which God had raised up the people called Methodist. He wrote on June 25, 1746:

> I would inquire . . . what is the end of all ecclesiastical order? Is it not to bring souls from the power of Satan to God, and to build them up in His fear and love? Order, then, is so far valuable as it answers these ends, and if it answers them not, it is nothing worth . . . And, indeed, wherever the knowledge and love of God are, true order will not be wanting. But the most apostolic order, where they are not, is less than nothing and vanity.[15]

This missional priority, this commitment to doing whatever was necessary to fulfill the mandate of the gospel, this willingness to modify even his basic ecclesiological understanding for the sake of the revival, brought Wesley to Bristol on September 1, 1784, and to the watershed decision to ordain.

Implications

It is not necessary here to go into detail in a history that is so well documented in other sources. Rather, we seek the reasons behind Wesley's decision to ordain in the Anglican pattern and the foundational principles that undergirded his ordinations.

First, the primary reason for the ordinations for America was the urgent need for sacramental ministry and ordered leadership among the people called Methodist in America. Wesley believed that the sacraments were an essential means of grace and consistently encouraged his people to regular, even daily, celebration of Holy Communion. He also believed in the principle that there was to be no sacramental administration without ordination. These two convictions led to Wesley's decision to ordain. The third motivating factor was the need. By the end of the American Revolutionary War, many of the Anglican priests had fled the country. The Methodist movement was spreading, and Wesley's admonition to seek the services of the Anglican Church for priestly ministry was entirely untenable. Asbury reported to Wesley that "thousands of children remained unbaptized in America, and that some members of the Methodist societies had not partaken of the Lord's Supper for many years."[16] This urgent need for the sacraments called for an ordained ministry among the Methodist people in America.

Second, Wesley followed the Anglican order because he felt that the polity of the Church of England was true to the New Testament and that the apostolic tradition was effective in providing ordered leadership for the church. Bishop William R. Cannon concludes that Wesley "sincerely believed that the episcopal form of government was the best form of church government."[17] He therefore ordained Whatcoat, Vasey, and Coke in that tradition and sent the liturgical provisions for such an ordering of ministry to the Methodists as the model for this new church. He wrote: "As our American brethren are now totally disentangled both from the State and from the British hierarchy, we dare not entangle them again either with the one or the other. They are now at full liberty simply to follow the Scriptures and the Primitive Church. And we judge it best that they should stand fast in that liberty wherewith God has so strangely made them free."[18] In order for them to fulfill this purpose, Wesley provided an ordered ministry that he believed to be in keeping with the apostolic and biblical tradition.

Third, the urgency of the call to preach and the inward call in the life of the preacher were central to the ministry of Wesley's preachers, whether lay or ordained Anglican clergy. It thus became a primary criterion for those seeking ordination and conference membership in the Methodist Episcopal Church in America and continues to be central to a Wesleyan understanding of ordained ministry.

Fourth, Wesley believed that the sacraments as a means of grace were central to the Christian life and that the necessity of an ordained ministry to administer them was foundational to a properly ordered church.

Fifth, there was a need for leadership in the church, which Wesley felt was best addressed through an episcopal form of ordination. He affirmed the threefold ordering of ministry, but believed that elder/presbyters and bishops were of the same order, differing only in function. Deacons shared the ministry of Word and Sacrament in a limited way and were ordained prior to elder's ordination.

Sixth, Wesley believed in the principle that the ministry ordains the ministry. That is, the authority and the tradition of the church, the faithful transmission of the faith, and the ordered life of the church were evidenced in a ministry where ordination is in the hands of the ordained. Wesley understood this pattern to follow the apostolic tradition as the way of extending the apostolic ministry into the future. Ordination through the laying on of hands by ordained leaders represented this apostolic history in a powerful and literal way.

Finally, all ordering of ministry was meant to fulfill the missional mandate of the gospel. Once again we see the pragmatic, mission-driven polity of the Methodist movement, rooted in Wesley's pragmatism and commitment to the mission of Christ as the overarching priority.

Francis Asbury, Philip William Otterbein, and Jacob Albright

Clearly, John Wesley's theology of ministry, growing out of his Anglican heritage combined with his evangelistic vision, formed the basic identity of the church in America. But what Wesley planted, Asbury shaped to fit the new context, giving it a distinct character, particularly in regard to the office of bishop and the pattern of itinerancy. Before we turn to Asbury it is important to note briefly one of the intervening events that led up to Wesley's ordinations for America and the Christmas Conference of 1784.

There were Methodist groups well established in the colonies twenty years before Wesley sent the plan for ordained ministers to provide the sacraments for them. Devereaux Jarrett was one of several ordained Anglican clergy in the colonies who served the Methodists during these years. He went from America to England to be ordained and understood Methodism not as "a new denomination, but as an evangelistic movement within the Anglican Church."[19] Many Methodist leaders, however, were lay preachers who were not ordained and yet felt the need for sacraments among their societies. For example, Robert Strawbridge insisted on his right to administer the sacraments, even after Thomas Rankin and Francis Asbury tried to dissuade him. In 1773 a conference of Methodist preachers called by Rankin faced the issue and affirmed their commitment to receive the sacraments only from ordained Anglican ministers,[20] but the issue was not resolved. It continued to ferment until the Fluvanna Conference.

Fluvanna Conference, 1779

The issue came to a crisis point in 1779.[21] Prior to the conference that was to be held at Broken Back Church, Fluvanna, Virginia, an irregular conference was called in Delaware. Ostensibly, it was held for the convenience of the northern preachers, but, in fact, the war made it unsafe for Asbury to travel to Virginia. Even more to the point, the irregular conference was called in hopes of preempting what was sure to happen in Fluvanna—the move toward separation from Wesley and the attempt to ordain clergy for sacramental ministry among Methodists.

The Delaware conference reaffirmed the desire to avoid separation from Wesley and proclaimed Asbury as his general assistant for America with clear Wesley-like authority concerning preachers and oversight of the church. The intent was to make certain that all the Methodists in America received sacraments only from properly ordained Anglican priests.[22]

The Fluvanna Conference moved in the opposite direction. The members appointed a presbytery with authority to examine and ordain preachers. This presbytery then proceeded to ordain themselves and a number of other preachers and to grant sacramental authority, an action that would have been found suspect even in the presbyterial denominations. The two conferences met again the next year, and the conference presided over by Asbury managed to persuade those who had been ordained in Fluvanna to withhold their administration until Wesley could provide a resolution. The breach was healed for the time being, but the issues remained.

Fluvanna was a critical turning point in the history and identity of Methodism. Had the Fluvanna Conference prevailed it would have posed a more serious theological and ecclesiastical problem than had Wesley's ordination since none of those doing the ordaining were ordained. It would not only have severed ties with Wesley and the Anglican tradition, but also with the apostolic tradition of the Christian church regarding ordination. Fluvanna demonstrated the tension in Methodism between an episcopal polity, represented by the superintendent/bishop, and a presbyterial form of church life, granting authority to the conference. This issue played a part in the schism led by James O'Kelly, the separation of the Methodist Protestants, and the creation of the Free Methodist and the Wesleyan Methodist churches and continues to be a point of tension today.

In summary, it is important to note that essentially both conferences of 1779 affirmed that sacramental administration required ordination, but Fluvanna dramatized the urgent need for sacraments among the Methodists in America as they moved toward the radical response of ordaining themselves and other ministers. In the end, these events affirmed the connection between sacrament and ordination, made clear that only the ordained would ordain, and helped to establish the authority of Francis Asbury as the people called Methodist moved toward the events of Christmas 1784.

The Christmas Conference, 1784

When Coke arrived in America in November 1784, he met with Francis Asbury at Barrett's Chapel. A crucial decision from that meeting shaped the future of Methodism. To Coke's surprise, Asbury insisted that Wesley's plan be approved by the conference and that he be ordained only if elected by the conference. Coke finally agreed, and the conference was called for Christmas Eve at Lovely Lane Church in Baltimore. Between November 14 and December 24 Coke went on a 900-mile horseback tour to get to know the Methodist congregations in America![23]

The Christmas Conference convened as planned, and the Methodist Episcopal Church was born. The members revised the British *Minutes*, thereby creating the first American *Discipline*, but they acknowledged loyalty to John Wesley as long as he lived. The decision to allow the conference to actually adopt Wesley's plan signaled the crucial role the conference would play in the life of Methodism to this day. Wesley's influence would continue to be felt during his lifetime, but, in fact, the respect granted him came from the action of the conference. The Methodist Episcopal Church was becoming an independent entity, born in the days of revolution and bringing together elements of episcopal and presbyterial administration.

Taking part in the ordination of Asbury was Thomas Coke, ordained a priest in the Anglican Church and a superintendent by Wesley, Thomas Vasey, and Richard Whatcoat, who had been ordained deacon and elder by Wesley; and Philip William Otterbein, an ordained German Reformed pastor. The fact that Asbury's and Otterbein's descendants would merge in 1968 to form The United Methodist Church gives added meaning to this moment.

Implications

What essential factors at work in these conferences shaped Methodist identity?

First, the need for the sacraments and the conviction that these could not be administered by persons who had not been ordained continued to be a driving force. The Christmas Conference followed Wesley in seeing a distinction between the preaching and the priestly offices, and they thereby affirmed the essential ministry of the lay preacher while reserving the priestly function for the ordained. The answer of the Fluvanna Conference was for the members to ordain themselves, which was theologically unacceptable and contrary to the Methodist identity. Wesley's answer and the action of the Christmas Conference was to establish a Methodist ordination so that Methodists could receive the sacraments from a properly ordained ministry, which included deacons and elders in the Anglican tradition but was distinctly Methodist in identity.

Second, the Christmas Conference affirmed a modified episcopal polity, as indicated by the fact that the members chose the name Methodist Episcopal and that Francis Asbury assumed the title of bishop rather than superintendent.[24] The conference accepted the threefold pattern of ordination, so Asbury and others were first ordained deacon, then elder; finally, Asbury was ordained bishop by persons who had already been ordained, upholding the apostolic tradition that the ministry appoints the ministry. Only later did Methodists use the term "consecration" for the setting apart of bishops, in order to make clear Wesley's conviction that elders and bishops are of the same order, but distinct in function.

And third, the authority of the superintendency (represented by Asbury), coupled with the fraternity of preachers in conference, became a basic pattern in Methodist order. The new church would seek to balance the authority of the bishop to ordain with the power of the conference to determine who should be received into the covenant community.

Asbury's understanding of ministry

David Steinmetz says, "It could conceivably be argued that Asbury's theology is nothing more than a homespun and simplified copy of Wesley."[25] Asbury was not Oxford trained; rather, he learned Hebrew on horseback and "had the plain man's interest in conclusions, not the scholar's fascination with arguments."[26] When challenged as to his authority as a bishop, Asbury responded: "I will tell the world what I rest my authority upon.

34

1. Divine authority. 2. Seniority in America. 3. The election of the General Conference. 4. My ordination by Thomas Coke, William Philip Otterbein, Richard Whatcoat, and Thomas Vasey. 5. Because the signs of an apostle have been seen in me."[27]

In the ordering of ministry in the Methodist Episcopal Church, Asbury followed Wesley's instructions, as adopted by the conference. He held to the threefold ministry of bishops, elders, and deacons, with a modified episcopacy. The authority of Methodist ministry was conferred by already existing ministries, with the first Methodist elders being ordained through Coke, representing the Anglican mother church, and Otterbein, representing the Reformation. These elders then set apart one of their number as bishop.

For Asbury, bishops, elders, and deacons shared in the ministry of Word and Sacrament. All shared equally in the ministry of Word; deacons, only partially in Sacrament. Deacons were seen as being a step below elders, but above local preachers. Bishops were of the same order as elders, but differed in authority. The bishop was elected for life by the conference and exercised final authority over the itineracy, a highly organized and uniquely Methodist system with strong, centralized control, for the purpose of spreading the gospel.

Itineracy and conference membership were the norm, with primary ministerial identity rooted in membership in the conference. There were two forms of ministry in the newly established church, traveling and local, with the governance of the church in the hands of the conference, which was comprised of the traveling ministry. Unordained preachers could be elected to membership in the conference if they agreed to itinerate. Traveling preachers who located could not vote in the conference, although, if ordained, they could still administer the sacraments. Local preachers who did not travel the circuits were not members of the conference, even if ordained.

For Asbury, itineracy was essential to the office of the bishop. He believed that "the work of an itinerant evangelist may not be the first duty of a bishop and it is certainly not the only duty, but it is nevertheless an indispensable task of any scriptural bishop."[28] He was also committed to itineracy as the best way to deploy preachers in order to fulfill the mission and accomplish the evangelistic task under ordered supervision by the bishop.

Finally, Asbury evaluated the validity of the Methodist order of ministry and justified the success of the Methodist Church in terms of the effective fulfillment of the church's mission to spread scriptural holiness.[29] With Wesley he believed that the final test was the proclamation of the gospel and the church's mission.

One of the gradual shifts under Asbury's leadership related to the church's understanding of sacramental administration and ordination. Though Asbury argued that sacraments could be celebrated only by properly ordained persons, Steinmetz says that "the sacramental aspect of ordination is the aspect which least interests Asbury."[30] His primary concern was the evangelistic task of the church. "Asbury's primary test of ministry," according to Thomas Frank, "was preaching, and the primary criterion for preaching was the ability to sway, convict and convert an audience.... This privileging of preaching, and particularly its removal from the context of liturgy and sacrament, had deep roots and would have far-reaching consequences for church polity." Frank notes that this was not new in Methodism, given the fact that Wesley saw his preachers as extraordinary messengers called solely to preach. "In the unstructured context of America, Methodist preachers felt complete freedom to ignore Wesley's Anglican liturgy for Sunday service and to neglect the Lord's supper."[31]

Jeffrey Mickle concludes: "If we were to characterize this emerging scheme, we would have to say that the *potesta iurisdictionis* (the power of jurisdiction centered in the various conferences), took priority over the *potesta ordinis* (the power of ordination, traditionally understood as Word and Sacrament). In fact, the two powers were somewhat disjoined insofar as some ministers only exercised their prerogatives under one of the two."[32]

Philip William Otterbein

Francis Asbury and Philip William Otterbein first met in 1774 when Asbury was 29 and Otterbein was 48. They built a lasting friendship, and, as we have noted, Otterbein took part in Asbury's ordination in 1784. They agreed that the evangelistic task and the spread of the revival were central, but disagreed on the form of organization that would be best suited to fulfill the tasks. Jeffrey Mickle's excellent article comparing their views of ministry is well worth careful review.[33]

The evolution of ministry in Otterbein's movement is not quite as easy to outline as that in Asbury's since by its very nature Otterbein's movement was less organized. In 1790 Otterbein called together seven clergy who represented Reformed, Mennonite, Amish, and Moravian traditions. The next year a slightly larger group met; however, the record of these meetings is incomplete. "Basically," Mickle says, "the group was not ecclesiastical; rather, it was a loosely organized group of preachers sharing a common interest in the growing revivalistic work."[34] Over the next decade an entity emerged that in 1800 became the United Brethren in Christ; however, until 1815 it functioned under unwritten rules from Otterbein. In these early days the fellowship was characterized by a desire to spread the revival. Members cooperated to that end, not necessarily to create a church, since each person maintained his denominational association. Therefore, the qualifications for admission to the ministry were the ability to preach and zeal for the revival, and the authority to administer the sacraments was reserved for those who had been ordained previously in their respective denominations. The members rejected excessive discipline beyond biblical guidelines and personal guidance from Otterbein.[35]

When the United Brethren in Christ was finally formalized in 1800, Otterbein and Martin Boehm were elected superintendents. They were not ordained or consecrated since elders and superintendents were of one order, set apart by one ordination. Otterbein did not use the title bishop, but was often referred to as father, reverend, or brother. In fact, "No ordinations were performed until October 2, 1813, when Otterbein ordained three of the long-time preachers as elders, six weeks before he died."[36]

As the United Brethren in Christ took on the polity of a church, the doctrine of ministry became clearer. Out of the Reformed tradition Otterbein's threefold pattern included two lay offices and a single order of ordained ministry. The ordained preacher had pastoral duties, administered the sacrament, and preached the Word. Lay elders were selected by the preacher for a lifelong office of disciplining and managing the affairs of the church. Lay deacons were elected annually by the congregation to care for the sick and the poor.

Local preachers and itinerant preachers shared equally in the conference. Superintendents differed from ordained preachers in function only and were elected to a four-year term. Itineracy and appointment making were essentially voluntary.

Primary governing authority was in the local church; however, authority to exercise ministries of Word and Sacrament was granted by the conference, not tied to the laying on of hands. For example, Christian Newcomer was elected a bishop before he was ordained by Otterbein. Ordination was done in the local church, and the certificate was issued in the name of the vestry, not the conference. The purpose of ordination was not sacramental or episcopal ministry, but for the sake of continuing the line of ordained clergy among the United Brethren. Ordaining seemed to be the only function reserved exclusively for ordained clergy.

Mickle notes that "unlike the disjunction between *potesta iurisdictionis* and *potesta ordinis* found in Methodism, the United Brethren maintained a unity between the two. All preachers were members of the annual conference, whether traveling or not. Thus, all members of the conference had the authority to preach, and all preachers in conference authorized individuals to preach, and/or baptize, and/or administer the Lord's Supper, and/or solemnize marriages. Sometimes all the sacramental prerogatives were granted; sometimes, only baptism was authorized; other times, an individual was allowed only to preach. . . . *Potesta ordinis* became a function of *potesta iurisdictionis:* the conference authorized the power of Word and Sacrament; that power did not rest on its own authority."[37]

The primary distinctions between Asbury and Otterbein and their respective movements involved the rigid demands of the

Discipline, the authority of the bishop, and the highly organized and centralized itinerant system of the Methodists, which the United Brethren saw as extreme and offensive. Mickle concludes:

> The difference between Asbury and Otterbein regarding the form of ministry is their basic point of orientation. Both men employ the conference of preachers as the main governing body of the connection. But, Asbury's basic orientation is from the episcopacy down; Otterbein's basic orientation is from the local congregation up . . . for Asbury, the conference modified a fundamental episcopalian orientation; for Otterbein, the conference modified a presbyterial foundation. . . . The norm for Asbury is the traveling, single, young man who goes from place to place on his circircuit preaching . . . exercising supervision . . . and, if ordained, administering the sacraments . . . all according to the detailed specifications in the *Discipline.* Asbury himself was the model *par excellence.* Otterbein, on the other hand, was a residential pastor, who traveled to other churches occasionally . . . The Baltimore Rules of 1785 presuppose the residential style of ministry. Itineracy became an optional form of ministry, but it was certainly not expected. . . . There were no rules laid down from above. . . . For Asbury, the ministry was most effective when the preachers followed the lead of the bishop as a celibate itinerant, bound by the rules of the conference. For Otterbein, the primary focus shifts to one based on circumstantial needs. Preacher-pastors are just as acceptable as preacher-itinerants.[38]

These differences evidence two very different ecclesiologies that shaped the two movements' understandings of ministry. For Asbury and the Methodists, church was conference—annual, quarterly, and eventually general. Preachers were sent to—not called to—the local congregation, and the local church was an expression of the connection, the conference. Otterbein began with the local congregation and built up.

Even though there were serious conversations between the Methodists and the United Brethren about coming together in the early 1800s, Asbury's modified Anglican episcopal polity was at odds with Otterbein's modified Reformed presbyterial form of governance. Over the years changes took place that brought the two churches closer together. The Brethren adopted a book of discipline and itinerancy. The Methodists became more pastoral and granted the local church a role in governance; but, as we will see in the discussion of specific changes in the new ordering of ministry in The United Methodist Church, "several of the significant issues that separated the modern descendants of these two men can be traced directly back to the differences between their doctrines of ministry."[39] This contrast can be seen in the Church today in the tension between connectionalism and congregationalism and in the growing emphasis on the local church in the *Book of Discipline.*[40]

Jacob Albright and the Evangelical Association

In 1813 Christian Newcomer assumed leadership of the United Brethren from Otterbein and worked for closer ties with the Methodists by drafting a discipline for the United Brethren, similar to the Methodist *Discipline.* Russell Richey notes, however, that he "intended his Discipline to serve as a basis for union not only with the Methodists but also with the other Methodist-like German denomination, the Evangelical Association."[41]

Jacob Albright experienced his own conversion and was nurtured in the faith in a Methodist class meeting. He became a class leader and licensed exhorter; but rather than identifying with the English-speaking Methodists, he began preaching in the German-speaking communities of Pennsylvania. Though he evidently never relinquished his credentials with the Methodists, Albright received little support from Asbury for the German-language work and felt the need for a separate conference in order to serve this population. However, Albright's movement among the Lutherans had closer ties to the Methodists than Otterbein's had. In fact, at their first formal conference in 1807, the members of Albright's movement called themselves the "newly formed Methodist Conference."

Albright appreciated the Methodist structure and discipline, but brought to it, as did Otterbein, the fervor of the German Pietist experience. By 1809 his followers referred to themselves as "those designated as Albright's people." The group finally settled on the name the Evangelical Association in 1816, and thus it remained for more than a century. Both the United Brethren and the Methodists sought union with the Evangelical Association from time to time, but that was not to be fully accomplished until 1968.

Jacob Albright and the Evangelical Association had a major impact on the Evangelical United Brethren tradition and on early Methodists. In some ways Albright represents a middle ground between Asbury and Otterbein. Like Asbury, Albright's theology was anchored in the Wesleyan movement and his polity focused on the conference structure. However, his understanding of the revival had a more congregational approach similar to Otterbein's. The Evangelical Association ordained both deacons and elders, often in immediate succession. They had bishops, but as William Lawrence notes, "they could function quite well without them. In fact, during the mid-nineteenth century they went decades without bothering to elect one to fill a vacancy."[42]

In their origins all three movements shared a common passion for evangelism and a polity that in various ways reflected the value of the conference. In terms of ministry, all three saw the maintenance of the revival and the spread of the gospel throughout the new American frontier as their mission. One might even suggest that the same missional pragmatism, a willingness to adapt forms to reach language groups and diverse communities, is reflected in their origins. The distinctions in terms of ordained ministry grew out of this pragmatism, coupled with the clear difference between Asbury's Anglican roots and the German Pietist and Reformed heritage of Otterbein and Albright.

In some ways I believe that these distinctions can be seen at work in the legislative changes of the 1996 General Conference. Though the differences between these historic streams were never used as argument for the new legislation, in fact the 1996 conference moved away from the Roman Catholic/Anglican tradition of Asbury to something that might be more akin to Otterbein's and Albright's Reformed tradition. At least, it is interesting to consider the new ordering of ministry in light of these three original movements.

41

Together, Albright, Otterbein, and Asbury represent the strands of tradition that comprise The United Methodist Church today and reflect the tensions as well as the synergy that brought us to our current ordering of ministry.

Tearing Apart, Coming Together

The Fluvanna Conference represented only the first of many tensions and divisions in the fabric of Methodism, all of which had implications for ordained ministry. The next major confrontation was led by James O'Kelly in 1787.

O'Kelly's republican Methodists

Only three years after the Christmas Conference, the issue of loyalty to John Wesley caused major division in the infant church. John Wesley sent word to Coke instructing that Richard Whatcoat be appointed as superintendent. In Virginia, James O'Kelly objected. At issue was Wesley's control vis-à-vis the authority of the conference and the role of the superintendency. Episcopal polity versus presbyterial governance was once again on the table. In Baltimore the conference rejected Whatcoat, "unceremoniously dropped the name of John Wesley from the designated superintendents. These actions vindicated Asbury as well as the conference."[43]

Two years later O'Kelly once again protested the centralized power of what was called the Council, a group of presiding elders selected by Asbury to lead the now eleven conferences. In 1792 a General Conference was called and the Council was disbanded; but on the second day of the conference, O'Kelly placed a motion that would have allowed preachers who felt they had been injured by an appointment to appeal to the conference and receive another appointment. His arguments likely would have connected with the new spirit of republicanism in the young nation in contrast to Wesley's authoritarian style of leadership and his obvious British identity. Once again the issue at hand was the balance of power between the bishop and the conference, particularly with regard to the itinerary.

Ultimately, O'Kelly's motion failed, and he and his followers walked out, unfortunately taking with them strong anti-slavery sentiments that were also part of their movement. Regrettably, this departure may have weakened the Methodist Episcopal Church's original abolitionist stance and opened the way for the divisions that were to come with regard to race. Most African American Methodists would ultimately withdraw to form separate denominations, and the church would divide regionally over the issue. In 1816 Richard Allen, an emancipated slave and Methodist preacher who had been present at the Christmas Conference, withdrew to form the African Methodist Episcopal Church (AME); and in 1821 the AME Zion Church was organized for African Americans who felt less than welcome in the Methodist Episcopal Church. Russell Richey confirms William Warren Sweet's estimate that the church lost about 10,000 members through the O'Kelly split and the other schisms of the 1790s,[44] but the call for a more egalitarian church continued to be raised.

Methodist Protestants

By the 1820s, the conference as the exclusive fraternity of traveling preachers was the focus of debate. Local preachers outnumbered traveling preachers three to one and formed the backbone of Methodist ministry in the local congregations, but were not members of the conference. They exercised their ministry under the supervision of the traveling preacher and the quarterly conference, and could be ordained deacon as of 1789 and elder as of 1812; however, the norms for the church were clearly itineracy and conference membership, not ordination.

There were three types of local preachers: those for whom it was a step on the way to itineracy, those for whom it was a permanent position, and those itinerant preachers who could no longer travel and were "located." All these were effectively outside the annual conference since membership and voting rights were reserved for traveling preachers. There was open questioning about the preference for traveling preachers and the role of local pastors in the conference, a debate that continues to be lively in the Church today.

The same arguments were being raised on behalf of laity. Should not laity as well as local preachers be represented in the annual conference? The pressure continued to build as the church moved toward 1824. The annual conference, which had originally been marked by its spiritual qualities, was becoming more politicized. As Russell Richey notes, "Debate over the prerogatives and boundaries of the fraternity had divided the fraternity. Acrimony operated as Gresham's Law, politicizing conferences and pressing out fraternity and revival. . . . There were to be no revivals associated with the General Conference of 1824."[45]

One issue to be resolved at the conference was the move to elect presiding elders. It was defeated by a vote of 63-61. By the same split votes, laity and local preachers were denied membership in the conference. While the conference met a number of reformers convened the Baltimore Union Society and founded a new periodical, *The Mutual Rights of Ministers and Members of the Methodist Episcopal Church,* calling for what they considered to be better balance in church government. In 1827 the reformers held a general convention with twenty-four societies represented. The regular conference of that year responded with expulsions of the breakaway leaders, but new congregations continued to join the reform movement. By 1830 they had organized twelve annual conferences; and in a General Conference they adopted a new constitution and discipline, elected Francis Waters as president, and took the name The Methodist Protestant Church. They accomplished the goals of an elected superintendency and lay representation, but local preachers were still not granted conference membership. The president would station the preachers, with appointments subject to revision by a conference committee. Unfortunately, the Methodist Protestants' concern for inclusion and equality did not extend to "coloured members." African Americans were denied vote and membership in the General Conference, and each annual conference was permitted to deal with the matter of race in its own way. Once again Methodists' unwillingness to hold fast to the strong anti-slavery convictions of Wesley and the Christmas Conference would be in evidence, and the seeds for future tension and division continued to be sown.

North and South

Although the Methodist movement at its inception was clearly opposed to slavery, the ways in which the Methodist Episcopal and Methodist Protestant churches compromised on matters of race caused numerous divisions and ultimately resulted in the most significant schism in our history. "Indeed," says Russell Richey, "four divisions can be traced directly to it, those represented by the Wesleyan Methodist Church, the Methodist Episcopal Church, South, the Free Methodists and the Colored Methodist Episcopal Church."[46] The Methodist Episcopal Church would divide North and South primarily over this issue; but much like the Civil War itself, other issues were also at work, including the understanding of ministry. The tension over slavery revealed once again the struggle between the authority of the conference and the role of the bishop; questions over the nature of the ministerial fraternity; the unity of the church versus the rights of individual clergy and/or bishops; regionalism versus the whole connection.

The struggle over slavery and abolition consumed the general conferences of the mid 1800s. Russell Richey details this history in chapter 10 of *The Methodist Conference in America*, which he entitles "Zion Divided Again."[47] In 1840 the Southerners won key battles and the stage was set for 1844. The questions posed by the slavery issue had a direct impact on issues of fraternity among clergy, the role of the episcopacy, and the authority of the conference over clergy practice. The case that became the focal point was that of Bishop James O. Andrew, who by marriage had become a slaveholder and by Georgia law was prohibited from manumission. After a week of intense debate the motion was made by William Capers to divide the church. The motion was referred to "the committee of nine on the division of the church." The resolution of the committee passed, and after adjournment the delegates from the slaveholding states met and called a convention for May 1, 1845, in Louisville, Kentucky.

In 1845 the Methodist Episcopal Church, South, was born, and "our beloved Zion" was split. "A Methodism that once would conference the continent now divided the people of God into a northern and southern kingdom. A Methodism that once had viewed its purposes in eschatological and biblical terms now reduced Zion to its own tribal ends and contested borders. Judah and Israel looked each to its own interest."[48]

Methodism was now divided in at least three ways. It was divided between Methodist Episcopal and Methodist Protestant over egalitarian issues; it was divided North and South over slavery; and the African American Methodists had broken away to create their own denomination. It would remain thus for almost a century, until 1939 when the Methodist Protestant, Methodist Episcopal, and Methodist Episcopal, South, churches reunited to become the Methodist Church.

Russell Richey suggests that through the stresses and strains of this history, the conference became more and more politicized, focusing on rights rather than on revival. The appeal to American political principles "made conference gatherings, both annual and general, very political affairs. . . . Much of the debate at this point became framed in terms of 'rights'—rights of conference, rights of the preachers, rights of the local preachers, rights of the laity."[49] It would appear that this notion of the purpose of the General Conference and the annual conference is still alive and well among us.

Coming together: The Methodist Church, 1939

The formation of the Methodist Church in 1939 and the goal of church unity included an attempt to bring balance between these traditions and the diverse understanding of ministry. The new *Discipline* affirmed the basic principles of ordained ministry in the new church. In summary, conference membership and itineracy were the norms, and the traveling preacher defined the ministry. The second category of ministry was the local ministry, identified by the fact that local preachers did not itinerate and were strictly local. Ordination could be granted to either traveling preachers or local preachers, but conference membershp was the defining mark. The call to preach continued to be the criterion for those who would join the ministry, either traveling or local. Women could serve as local preachers, but were not admitted to the traveling ministry. Though sacramental administration was not directly addressed as a major issue, the norm was still for sacraments to be administered by the ordained. The church allowed an unordained pastor to "administer the Sacrament of Baptism and the Lord's Supper in the bounds of his own Charge, in the absence of the District Superintendent, with the understanding that no permanent powers of ordination are conferred until granted by the laying on of hands after he has met the Disciplinary requirements."[50]

There was no clear definition of ordination, but the merged church followed the tradition that deacons were granted authority to preach, conduct worship, perform marriages, baptize, and assist the elder with the Lord's Supper. After serving as a local deacon for four years or following two years of service as a supply pastor after being ordained deacon, one could be ordained elder with full sacramental authority.

In regard to the setting apart of bishops, the 1939 *Discipline* struck a creative compromise by using both the words *ordain* and *consecrate* to describe the action. It read, "The Bishops shall be elected by the respective Jurisdictional and Central Conferences and ordained or consecrated in the historic manner of Episcopal Methodism."[51]

The new church attempted to satisfy the concerns of the Methodist Protestant Church by including laity in the annual conference. The concerns of the Methodist Episcopal Church, South, regarding regional character and segregation were acknowledged in the creation of jurisdictional conferences and the Central Conference for African Americans, effectively keeping segregation in place. Once again the church missed the opportunity to reclaim the original convictions of Wesley and the Christmas Conference, and the divisions over race were firmly established in the central conference structure.

By 1939 Methodist ministry had been reshaped by the transitions it had endured. The recurring themes represented in the schisms of O'Kelly, the Methodist Protestants, and the

North/South split are important to the evolution of Methodism since many of these issues continue to impact our ordering of ministry today. Of the many implications that can be drawn from this brief history, I would suggest the following:

First, the understanding of ministry in Methodism continued to be a pragmatic and functional response to the needs of the time, but, whereas Wesley's and Asbury's pragmatism was in response to a clear evangelistic mandate and the sacramental need, many of the later decisions were in response to the political, geographic, and social struggles that were at work in the church. Perhaps it is not unfair to say that it became political pragmatism rather than mission-driven pragmatism that motivated the decisions about the ordering of ministry and polity.

Second, sacramental administration continued to decrease as a driving force in decisions about ministry. The call to preach and the willingness to itinerate continued to take precedence. The pragmatic response to the need for sacraments was to permit unordained persons to administer them where an ordained person was not available. Though it did meet an important missional need, this issue strained the relationship between ordination and sacramental administration and can be compared with the changes of 1996, which include an ordination without sacramental authority and the broader use of non-ordained local pastors with sacramental authority.

Third, ordination seemed to lose importance as conference membership and itinerancy became the norms. Little was said in the 1939 *Discipline* about ordination, its purpose, meaning, and relationship to conference membership, whereas much attention was given to the nature of itinerancy and conference membership.

Fourth, bishops were to be ordained or consecrated and continued to be charged with presidential responsibility, spiritual oversight, and the administration of appointive itinerancy. The fact that they were now elected jurisdictionally and not by the general church tended to weaken their role as bishops for the whole church.

Finally, the inclusion of the Methodist Protestant commitment to lay empowerment resulted in lay membership in the annual conference. This marked a significant turning point in both the nature and the purpose of the annual conference and of the covenant community of clergy in full connection. Laity could not vote on matters of ordination and character of ministers, and the clergy covenant was maintained in the executive session; but annual conference took on a new meaning in Methodism at this time. The issue of the rights of laity and the balance of power continues to be a major force into the present and is reflected in the 1996 legislation and in the debates that have followed.

So the coming together of these three strands of Methodism represented a welcome reunion of a broken family. In many ways it affirmed the central traditions and practices of the people called Methodist, the children of Wesley and Asbury, Fluvanna and Baltimore, O'Kelly and Bishop James Andrew. Unfortunately, it did not include African Americans in full participation. The compromises continued de facto segregation and failed to proclaim and live out the inclusive stance of Wesley and the first generation of Methodists. It included the seeds of future tension and unresolved issues, but also represented Methodism's ongoing, pragmatic desire to do what seemed best for the fulfillment of the church's mission in the world.

Coming together: The United Methodist Church, 1968

On April 23, 1968, Bishop Reuben Mueller and Bishop Lloyd C. Wicke joined hands and said, "Lord of the Church, we are united in thee, in Thy Church and now in the United Methodist Church." Thus was born The United Methodist Church, bringing together the heirs of Wesley and Asbury with the sons and daughters of Otterbein and Albright. The various Methodist branches had reunited in 1939, and in 1946 the Evangelical Church and the United Brethren Church had merged to form the Evangelical United Brethren (EUB). The journey toward union that Asbury and Otterbein had discussed almost 200 years earlier was finally fulfilled in 1968.

Prior to the uniting conference, in 1966 a special conference of the Methodist Church received a report from the study committee on the ministry. The substantive change was to replace the term "traveling preacher in full connection" with "effective full-time ministerial member" because it was felt this would permit more flexibility for the study committee as they prepared for the union. As Richard Heitzenrater notes, "What is lost in that change are the basic concepts of *itineracy* and *connectionalism!* Nevertheless, that tentative change was felt to be necessary at the time."[52]

In the report to the uniting conference in 1968, the study committee carefully and intentionally reaffirmed the link between orders and sacrament. Only ministers (in the restrictive sense, meaning ordained clergy) were permitted to administer the sacraments. Heitzenrater notes, "Walter Muelder emphasized in the discussion on the floor of the conference that there is a fundamental distinction between laity and ordained clergy, that this distinction is related precisely to the question of the administration of the sacraments, and that this distinction is 'absolutely fundamental.' "[53] Therefore, lay pastors, the new term for approved supply pastors were not authorized to celebrate the sacraments. Clearly, this was in keeping with the theological understanding of Wesley, Asbury, and Otterbein and followed the historic practice of the church. The study committee believed that it also placed the new denomination in the mainstream of the ecumenical movement. The direct and immediate effect, however, was to prevent unordained local pastors from administering the sacrament, "the first time such a situation existed . . . since 1926 in the [Methodist Episcopal Church,] South and 1939 in the unified church."[54] This restriction held for only one quadrennium, when the Church realized that, in practice, some provision for local pastors to provide sacramental ministry was essential to many congregations. However, it did represent the attempt of the uniting conference to take seriously the connection between ordination and sacrament.

The new church retained two orders of ordained ministry, following the pattern Wesley had adopted from the Anglican Church, even though the former members of the Evangelical United Brethren came to the table with one ordination. Elders were defined as "ministers who have completed their formal preparation for the ministry of Word, Sacrament, and Order; [and]

50

have been elected itinerant members in full connection with an Annual Conference." Deacons were clearly defined as preparatory elders, with no emphasis being placed on a ministry distinct from the elder: "Deacons are ministers who have progressed sufficiently in their preparation for the ministry to be received by an Annual Conference as either probationary members or associate members."[55]

The latter was a new creation of the 1968 conference in response to the need to deal with the status of EUB pastors who were not ordained elders. Associate members would be ordained deacon as a terminal ordination. They were, in fact, "permanent deacons" (a term frequently used today to refer to deacons in full connection). The office was discontinued in the 1996 legislation, but numerous associate member deacons continue to serve in the Church and will be present for the foreseeable future.

Local pastors were clearly identified as "laymen duly licensed to preach."[56] Another lay office created for the new church was the lay worker, defined as "a person other than the clergy whose decision to make a career of work (either full-time or term) in the employed status in the Church or church-related agencies is accompanied by the meeting of standards of excellence in the chosen field of service and who has been consecrated by a bishop."[57] This marked a significant step toward what was to become the office of diaconal minster in 1976 and ultimately to evolve into the new ordained deacon in full connection.

Given the legislative changes of 1996, it is interesting to note the use of the terms "commissioning" and "consecration" in the 1968 legislation. The lay worker was to be consecrated, a liturgical act that was permitted to be part of the ordination service. But they were also commissioned: "A lay worker shall be commissioned, *i.e.*, entrusted with work in a particular task in which a consecrated lay worker is to serve. The service of commissioning and any subsequent related act of installation or convenantal relationship with the employing church or church-related body shall be arranged in consultation with the certifying agency."[58] Obviously, juxtaposition of terms and confusion between consecration and commissioning were not new to 1996.

Regarding the role of women, the new church followed the pattern of the former United Brethren from 1889 until their merger with the Evangelical Church in 1946 and the commitment of the Methodist Church since 1956 to include women in the ordained ministry. In the new United Methodist Church "both men and women are included in all provisions of the *Discipline* which refer to the ministry."[59] The uniting conference also did away with the Central Jurisdiction for African Americans, which had effectively institutionalized segregation in the former Methodist Church. It was an important, though long overdue, step in rectifying the years of discrimination and moving the Church closer to the passionate stance of John Wesley and the first Methodist conference in America.

The compromises and accommodations made by the 1968 uniting conference created a church that favored Methodist history in its strong insistence on the connection between ordination and sacraments and in the provision for elders and deacons, yet provided for the needs of the EUB Church through the office of associate member. The term "minister" related to ordained clergy, and a clear distinction was made between ministers and laity, focused in sacramental authority. Opportunities for laity to serve in the professional ministry of the Church were provided through the offices of local pastor and lay worker. Conference membership continued to take precedence over ordination as the defining relationship, and itineracy was reaffirmed as an essential component of conference membership and ordination. With some modifications, most noticeably the creation of the diaconal ministry in 1976, this basic pattern of ministry remained in place until 1996.

CHAPTER TWO

Ordination Within the Ministry of All Christians

The ministry of all Christians consists of service for the mission of God in the world. The mission of God is best expressed in the prayer that Jesus taught his first disciples: Thy kingdom come; thy will be done, on earth as in heaven. All Christians, therefore, are to live in active expectancy: faithful in service of God and their neighbor; faithful in waiting for the fulfillment of God's universal love, justice, and peace on earth as in heaven.
—*The Book of Discipline,* ¶ 110

The first time I spoke on the floor of the General Conference was in 1984. I was a reserve delegate, but Carl Price knew that as a member of our Board of Ordained Ministry, I had a particular interest in the ministry legislation and graciously relinquished his seat so I could be on the floor for this discussion. The proposal called for the term "minister" to refer to all Christians, not just to ordained clergy. Because we were referring the whole study of ministry to yet another study committee, I spoke in favor of including this matter in the referral in order to have a full and complete study of all aspects of ministry. The General Conference approved the new definition of the ministry and the minister. At the time, I doubt I realized the importance of this discussion, which signaled another significant transition in the evolution of

United Methodist ministry. It was a remarkable turnaround from only two quadrennia earlier when the General Conference took exactly the opposite position, defining a minister as an ordained person.[1]

This change in definition represented an emphasis on the ministry of the *laos,* which has emerged in almost every denomination in recent years. Specifically for United Methodists, it is probably fair to say that at that time it also served to undergird the calling of laity serving in the specialized ministry of the newly created office of diaconal minister, but the emphasis on ministry as the work of the whole church was in keeping with the emerging ecumenical consensus and has continued to reshape the ministry of our Church throughout these decades.

Ministry as the Work of the Whole People of God

The consensus document adopted by the World Council of Churches in 1982, *Baptism, Eucharist and Ministry,* defines ministry as the calling of the whole people of God. It states, "All members are called to discover, with the help of the community, the gifts they have received and to use them for the building up of the Church and for the service of the world to which the church is sent. . . . The word *ministry* in its broadest sense denotes the service to which the whole people of God is called."[2] This landmark document serves as the foundation for ecumenical consensus and for reflection on our own ministry and is consistent with the intent of the study of the ministry that the Council of Bishops brought to the 1996 General Conference.

Bishop David Lawson, one of the chief architects of the bishops' report said that the foundation of the bishops' proposal was the ministry of the laity. We were convinced that this issue was as confused as any other. Our vision was of millions of United Methodist members, each with an identity of personal Christian ministry, moving in their spheres of influence in the name of Jesus Christ. It was the desire to release this spiritual power that produced the ideas in that report."[3] The bishops' vision was that any ordering of ordained ministry would have as its focus the enhancement of the ministry of the whole Church, helping every Christian to see his or her work and life as an avenue of Christian witness and service. One of the purposes of ordination would be to equip and enhance the full scope of ministry. The bishops emphasized that ordained clergy are not set apart only to minister, but also to call forth, to lead, and to equip the whole church for witness and service in the world.

Lay Ministry in the United Methodist Tradition

For Methodists this emphasis on the ministry of all Christians should come as a familiar theme. The Wesleyan revival in England and the Methodist movement in America were, by and large, a lay movement. Wesley assumed the presence of ordained Anglican clergy and expected that the people called Methodist would rely upon them for the priestly functions. He called upon lay preachers and unordained class leaders to spread the revival through preaching and caregiving ministries in the world. All Methodists were expected to live lives of witness and service; only the priestly, sacramental ministries were reserved for the ordained. James Garlow notes that "Wesley appealed to several theological traditions, among them Presbyterian, Roman Catholic and his own Church of England as evidence that laypersons could legitimately minister."[4]

In his "A Farther Appeal to Men and Religion," Wesley drew on colorful rhetoric to defend the ministry of the laity:

> Why, must not every man, whether Clergyman or layman, be in some respects like the Apostles or go to hell? Can any man be saved if he be not holy, like the Apostles: a follower of them, as they were of Christ? And ought not every preacher of the gospel to be in a peculiar manner like the Apostles, both in holy tempers, in exemplariness of life and in his indefatigable labours for the good of souls . . . making full proof of his ministry in spending and being spent for Christ?[5]

Specifically, Wesley argued at great length for the ministry of the lay preacher. After confronting the protest, "But they are laymen," he referred to the Old Testament scribes, who were not priests, and even to the example of Jesus Christ: "The Jews themselves never objected to Our Lord's preaching even though he was not a priest after Aaron."[6] He pointed out that no one objected to the fact that the apostles were not priests and focused on Acts 8, writing that "all were scattered abroad and went everywhere preaching the Word." Wesley concluded, "Now what shadow of reason have we to think that all these were ordained before preaching?"[7]

Though Wesley held a high view of ordination, there was, as Harold Burgess says, no "clerical monopoly of the ministry of grace."[8] Wesley's use of laypersons in every aspect of ministry represents one of the best applications of the principle of the ministry of all Christians in the history of the Church. Laity took on the ministry of preaching, teaching, evangelism, caregiving, community service, and overseeing the spiritual life of bands, classes, and societies.

In their detailed review of local preachers in British Methodism, Geoffrey Melburn and Margaret Batty trace the ways in which laity have ministered in British Methodism. Today every circuit includes trained, unpaid local preachers who regularly fill the pulpits and serve in a multitude of ways in the congregation and beyond. Melburn and Batty acknowledge that there has been confusion as to the nature of the local pastor, whether "order, office, ministry, status, or leadership."[9] But the effectiveness of this lay ministry has never been questioned. Persons from all walks of life, including members of Parliament, have been British local preachers, and women have long been included. Mary Bosanquet (1739–1815), for example, was an ardent Methodist and notable preacher, the wife of the Rev. John Fletcher, an outstanding leader in early British Methodism. Local preacher Arthur Henderson (1863–1935) is another example; he was a labor leader, M.P., and statesman who won the Nobel Peace Prize in 1934.

As we have already seen, the planting of Methodism in pre-revolutionary America predated the sending of the persons ordained by Wesley in 1784. Following the revolution the absence of Anglican clergy called for the ordination of persons to provide sacramental ministry and ordered leadership for the fledgling church, but the backbone of Methodism as a movement was the ministry of laypersons as local preachers, exhorters, and class leaders who carried the Methodist movement far beyond the reach of the traditional clergy.

As settlements on the American frontier grew into established communities, the traveling preachers began to settle as well, replacing local preachers as pastors of local congregations. Ministry became more professionalized, and more of the actual function of ministry rested on the clergy. Laity came to assume that professional clergy would do ministry for them rather than lead the whole church in fulfilling its calling. For Methodists, the emphasis on the servant ministry (*diakonia*) of the whole church (the *laos*) is a recovery of our historic understanding of ministry.

Forms of Professional Lay Ministry

Lay ministries have been affirmed through a variety of full-time and part-time, paid and volunteer offices in the Church, including exhorters, stewards, class leaders, lay leaders, Sunday school superintendents, and certified lay workers. These voluntary forms of leadership have always been significant forms of service and leadership. In more recent years, various forms of lay ministry have emerged for persons who felt called to serve vocationally in leadership roles in the Church as a career.

There is probably no finer example of this vision for the ministry of all Christians than the life of Harry Denman. The son of a foundry worker who emigrated from England, Denman was born in Birmingham, Alabama, in 1893. When he was nine years old his father left the family, and Harry dropped out of school and went to work as an errand boy for the Tennessee Coal and Iron Company. He worked in the company until 1915, when he became the secretary for the Birmingham Sunday School Council for the monthly salary of $30, on which he supported his mother and family. From those humble beginnings God formed a powerful leader for the cause of Christ who shaped the future of evangelism in the Methodist movement, first as secretary of education in the Methodist Episcopal Church, South, then as general secretary of the Board of Evangelism in the Methodist Church until his retirement in 1965. His ministry continued through preaching and letter writing until he died on November 8, 1976. Untold thousands heard him preach or were blessed by his letters, and many more were won to Christ through the work of the Board of Evangelism and the Upper Room under his leadership.

One story from his ministry describes his passion and power as a lay preacher. In 1958 he preached at the National Convocation on Local Church Evangelism in Washington, D.C., and concluded with the story of a bishop in his area reading the appointments:

> A church was to have a new preacher appointed as pastor. The members of that church had a beautiful sanctuary; they had a lovely educational building; they had a parking lot. I think they had air conditioning. They had a beautiful kitchen, lovely recreational facilities, an outdoor barbecue place. They had everything, even a little debt! The talk of the conference was "Who's going to be the pastor of this church? Who is the bishop going to send?" A good many were willing to go, to put themselves on the altar! The name of the church was Calvary!

He reached the climax of all he wanted to say, thundering,

> WHO WANTS TO GO TO CALVARY? WHO WANTS TO GO TO TELL ABOUT A SAVIOR, TO TELL ABOUT THE GOOD NEWS OF GOD, TO TELL ABOUT ETERNAL LIFE, TO TELL ABOUT THE KINGDOM OF GOD? WHO WANTS TO GO TO CALVARY TONIGHT?[10]

With that kind of conviction and persuasion, Denman led the Church, in both evangelism and social witness, through a time of dramatic growth, and he did it all as a layman. For Denman and for the clergy with whom he served, there was no question about the validity of his ministry or the significance of theirs. Together with other laity, bishops, and ordained clergy, he modeled a mutuality of ministry long before the contemporary emphasis on the ministry of all Christians was in vogue. Denman's ministry modeled the task of all who claim the name of Christ to carry the gospel to others, to represent Christ in the world, and to serve in the marketplace as well as the sanctuary. In the forward to his biography, Billy Graham calls him "one of the great mentors for evangelism in my own life and ministry—and for countless others in evangelism as well."[11]

These examples of various forms of lay leadership in Methodist practice highlight the important ministry of laity throughout our history. Forms have come and gone (the exhorter and the diaconal minister, for example), but the need to find avenues for laity, both volunteer and professional, to serve in specialized ministries remains. In the proposals the bishops prepared for the 1996 General Conference, they recommended the creation of the lay ministry steward as an office for laity who provide spiritual leadership in the local church. Though rejected by the General Conference, it represented an attempt to take this ministry seriously. With a renewed emphasis on the ministry of all Christians as the underlying theme in the new ordering of ministry, I believe that we will find new ways of affirming these various ministries, representative of the ministry that is entrusted to all through baptism.

Deaconess

Perhaps the most vivid example of lay ministries of service in the community is the deaconess. As early as 1736 Wesley, then an Anglican priest serving in Georgia, appointed three deaconesses in his Georgia mission to assist in caring for the sick. This appointment, in fact, led to one of the charges brought against him that forced his hasty departure from the colony.[12] Today deaconesses are commissioned by the Board of Global Ministries "to express representatively the love and concern of the believing community for the needs in the world and to enable, through education and involvement, the full ministry and mission of the people of God" (¶ 1313). Though currently few in number in the United States, deaconesses continue a vital ministry of laywomen who are called to service in the world. The deaconess is stronger in Methodism in other parts of the world, as exemplified in the deaconess program in the Philippines. With the Church's decision no longer to consecrate diaconal ministers, perhaps we will see increased interest in this office by laywomen who sense a call to these specialized ministries of service. In function and mission the deaconess is one of the best models for the vision of the ministry of the ordained deacon in full connection as defined by the 1996 legislation, but the office of deaconess continues to lift up the calling of laity to specialized ministries of service in the world in Christ's name.

Diaconal minister

The office of diaconal minister was created in 1976 for the express purpose of affirming the calling and ministry of laypersons serving as professionals in the Church. It grew out of the earlier office of certified lay worker and for twenty years offered a means for the "recognition of their calling, skills, and professional rights and responsibilities"[13] of these persons. Diaconal ministers were consecrated; and though there was confusion about their identity, this office provided an avenue for diverse lay ministries to be celebrated by the Church. About half of the 1,500 diaconal ministers have now been ordained deacons, and the number of diaconal ministers in service will continue to diminish. Their ministry through these few decades, nevertheless, needs to be celebrated. Some of the central conferences have similar offices, for example, the *Gemeindereferentinnen* in Germany, offering an identifiable office for lay professionals in the Church.

Diaconal ministers modeled the conviction that one did not have to be ordained to be in the ministry of the Church, but tension about their relationship to laity on one hand and clergy on the other created confusion and contributed to the call to identify these ministries as a form of ordained clergy rather than as laity. For many diaconal ministers the creation of the deacon in full connection, identified as clergy, comes as the fulfillment of their original calling and their understanding of diaconal ministry in its inception. But the change also means that we no longer have a category for laity serving the Church in specialized ministry as a professional career.

Certification in professional ministry careers

For many years a variety of professional ministry careers have been certified by the Board of Higher Education and Ministry (¶ 426.19-20). Though certification can be granted to both clergy and laity, this program has frequently been used to train and affirm the calling and work of laity serving in the local church. Under the new ordering of ministry, certification provides the opportunity for training and authorization of diverse ministries, including Christian education, youth, evangelism, music, and business management. The Division of Ordained Ministry's Section of Deacons and Diaconal Ministries is currently taking specific steps to strengthen and revise this program in order to serve the Church more effectively and to undergird lay ministry in local churches.

Missionary

Without a doubt, the ministry of persons in mission through the Board of Global Ministries has been one of the truly transformative ministries of the Church. Inclusive of both laypeople and clergy, missionaries sent by the Church both within the nation and around the world have modeled the global vision of the Church and fulfilled diverse ministries of service and witness in the name of Christ.

As a college student, my own sense of call was deeply influenced by the many missionaries whose powerful model for the ministry touched my life. One who modeled this commitment in life and death was Burleigh Law; his story is told by his widow in the book *Appointment Congo*. Law served in the Congo during the early 1960s, years of turmoil leading up to revolution and independence. He was killed while trying to land his plane in order to assist other missionaries in their evacuation. He was a layperson, a mechanic by trade, and more than once he struggled with the all too common assumption that to be called by God for ministry meant one had to be ordained. It was clear, however, that his calling was as a lay missionary. He became so loved and respected by the people he served that he was "named by the Congolese 'Leopard Chief of the Artisans,' which meant that the people understood he was there to serve with his hands."[14] Around the world, missionaries have used the diverse gifts of laity to carry out the Great Commission, serving with their hands in the name of Christ.

Lay speaker

The lay speaker program certifies persons with specific training "in witnessing to the Christian faith through spoken communication, church and community leadership, and care-giving ministries" (¶ 270.1). Designed primarily for volunteers, the program is supervised by the Board of Discipleship, and training is usually offered through the district. Lay speakers provide for leadership in the local church as well as throughout the district and have been used, particularly in some ethnic minority and small membership churches, to provide lay leadership and preaching ministries. Their ministry is similar to the role of the lay preacher in British Methodism and carries on the historic Methodist ministry of the exhorter, class leader, and lay preacher.

Lay missioner

A recent addition to the ordering of ministry, this position is specifically related to the National Plan for Hispanic Ministries. Mostly volunteers, the missioners work under the guidance of a pastor to "develop faith communities, establish community ministries, develop church school extension programs, and engage in congregational development" (¶ 274). We can hope that this concept will be expanded in the future to serve in other communities, in addition to those served by the National Plan for Hispanic

Ministries, as a means of evangelism, church planting, and small group ministry. It could become an important avenue for lay ministry and outreach, particularly in communities that cannot afford the salaries of ordained deacons or elders. The role of the missioner is reminiscent of that of Wesley's class leaders and lay preachers who formed the backbone of the Methodist revival.

The category of lay missioner has provided the opportunity for laity to give leadership in the development of faith groups and to strengthen existing congregations. The report of the National Plan for Hispanic Ministries to the 2000 General Conference states, "By mid-1999, a total of 796 lay missioners and 100 pastor-mentors, representing 46 annual conferences, had been trained for ministry with Hispanics."[15] Lay missioners are trained and mentored by pastors and help to form faith communities for Bible study, worship, and prayer as well as serving in outreach ministries. One of those lay missioners is Felicidad Santiago, from Queens, New York. She serves "in a ministry of compassion that few in her church would consider. After her training, she began working in an ecumenical program in the Bronx that seeks to rehabilitate women addicted to drugs and/or alcohol. Her ministry involves visiting and counseling women of different ages, and taking them to hospitals and government offices that provide them and their families with assistance. Sharing God's love with women addicted to drugs or alcohol is a challenging ministry. . . ."[16]

Some lay missioners have felt called to ordained and licensed ministry in the Church and have moved on to become candidates for service as missionaries, deacons, elders, and local pastors. The lay missioner provides an opportunity for laypersons to be trained and mentored and to serve in the outreach of the Church and the building up of the body of Christ.

Ministry of All Christians Today

The Council of Bishops' report to the 1996 General Conference was based on a strong affirmation of the ministry of all Christians and emphasized the role of the ordained in equipping and leading baptized Christians in ministry. Out of that work the 1996 *Book of Discipline* clearly affirms baptism as the foundation of all ministry. In some of its most inspiring passages, the *Discipline* says:

> All Christians are called to this ministry of servanthood in the world to the glory of God and for human fulfillment. The forms of this ministry are diverse in locale, in interest and in denominational accent, yet always catholic in spirit and outreach. (¶ 104)

> Beyond the diverse forms of ministry is this ultimate concern: that all persons will be brought to a saving relationship with God through Jesus Christ and be renewed after the image of their creator (Colossians 3:10). This means that all Christians are called to minister wherever Christ would have them serve . . . (¶ 105)

> The people of God, who are the church made visible in the world, must convince the world of the reality of the Gospel or leave it unconvinced. There can be no evasion or delegation of this responsibility; the church is either faithful as a witnessing and serving community, or it loses its vitality and its impact on an unbelieving world. (¶ 107)

Howard Belben reminds us that the word "ministry in the New Testament is *diakonia,* which also means service. This ministry belongs to the whole church." He notes that unfortunately, "we tend to use the word 'minister' closer to the term 'klerikos' or 'clergy,' rather than 'diakonos.' "[17] This contributes to the confusion between the ministry of the whole people of God (*diakonia*) and the set-apart ministry of the ordained (*klerikos*).

In a recent Alban Institute book *Ministry for a New Time,* James Fenhagen raises some of the theological issues inherent in our concepts of ordination and lay ministry. His view of the Episcopal Church at this juncture is probably true of Methodism as well. He says:

> For the past twenty years, the creative and progressive energy of the Episcopal Church has been centered around the recovery of

the ministry of the laity . . . affirmed the communal and non-hier-
archical nature of the church given to us in baptism and affirmed
in an understanding of the Eucharist, where the priesthood of the
people of God stands at the center of the church's self-offering in
Christ. The theological problem that has emerged as a result of our
increasing clarity about the ministry of the laity is an increasing
lack of clarity about the ministry of the clergy. The truth is we are
living in a theological time lag. Our theology of baptism reflects a
vision of the church that is in conflict with our theology of ordination and the structures and symbols by which this theology is
communicated.[18]

In United Methodism we quickly adopted a new definition of
ministry and minister to reflect this theology of the *laos,* but the
need for clarity about the role of ordained clergy within the ministry of the *laos* is urgent.

As we have already seen from the early days of the Methodist
movement, there has been tension over the relationship between
lay and ordained ministries as evidenced in the James O'Kelly
revolt. The balance of power between laity and clergy was a
major factor leading to the creation of the Methodist Protestant
Church. Today, that same struggle underlies debates about various aspects of ordination, the role of the local pastor, and the
place of laity in the approval process for ordination. All too often
a theology of ministry and mission gets lost in the political
process, and representation becomes more important than theology or calling. As important as shared power and representation-
al polity may be, they dare not take precedence over the call to
shared ministry for the sake of the world and the proclamation of
the gospel.

Perhaps the most obvious warning about the potential conflict
between ordained and lay ministries in the 1996 ministry legislation is found in the requirements for the appointment of deacons
in full connection. Deacons are required to present "a written
statement of intentionality of servant leadership in order to establish a clear distinction between the work to which all Christians
are called and the work for which deacons in full connection are
appropriately prepared and authorized" (¶ 322.4*b*). This require-

ment is related to the deacon since any ministry done by the deacon is also appropriate for a layperson; however, this clear distinction is important for all ordinations lest we undercut the ministry of laity by further clericalization of the ministry.

Assuming that we approach the question of ordination with a prior commitment to ministry (*diakonia,* service) as the work of the whole church, the basic question then becomes "Why ordain?" The question is both functional and theological: not only, "For what functions are persons set apart by ordination?" but also, "What does ordination as deacon or elder mean in the life of the Church?"

Foundations for Ordination Within the Ministry of All Christians in Methodism

From our earlier review of our founders and our tradition, the following elements emerge as central to our historical understanding of the distinction between lay and ordained ministry and the rationale for ordination.

Calling

Wesley specifically required that his preachers have a clear sense of the "inward call." That personal call was to be confirmed by the "outward call" of the church; but in his day emphasis on the inward calling, the personal sense of God's invitation and intervention in the life of the preacher, was unique to the Methodists. As the pattern for Methodist ordination was established in America, this emphasis on the inward call became a part of the expectation for candidates for ordination. In the movements that ultimately came together to form contemporary United Methodism, Otterbein stressed this inward call for his followers; and Asbury demanded that those who sought ordination experience a definite call to preach, which would be confirmed by the conference. The personal inward calling and the outward call of the church formed the basis for setting apart persons for ordained ministry.

Sacraments

In United Methodism's antecedent bodies, sacramental authority was always entrusted to ordained clergy. For Wesley, laity could carry out every other aspect of ministry, including preaching; but the priestly functions were reserved for the ordained. Asbury's primary concern was not sacramental ministry, but he assumed that the sacraments would be administered by ordained persons. Otterbein was more presbyterial, with the conference granting sacramental administration as needed; but one of the functions associated with ordination was sacramental ministry.

Early in the life of both the British Methodist Church and the Methodist Episcopal Church, pragmatic missional necessity led to the granting of limited sacramental authority to unordained local preachers in specific settings for a limited period of time under the supervision of an ordained minister. For a time American Methodism addressed this need through the ordination of local deacons and local elders. When these offices were discontinued local pastors were granted limited sacramental rights through the license. Given the permission granted these laypersons to administer the sacrament, it is obvious that sacramental administration has not always *required* ordination; but before 1996 ordination always *included* sacramental ministry. More will be said on this in a later section. For now, we can identify sacramental ministry as one of the primary functions authorized by ordination.

Word

Ordination has always represented the apostolic task of the faithful transmission of the faith and the proclamation of the Word. Though preaching did not require ordination, ordination has always included the ministry of the Word. In Methodism, and in Protestantism in general, this ministry is primarily fulfilled in the preaching ministry, but also includes diverse ways in which God's Word is proclaimed and the faith is communicated in the world.

Order

The word *order* was not added to the formula for ordination until the creation of The United Methodist Church in 1968. Ordination has always, however, included responsibility for ordering the ministry of the church. Wesley's decision to ordain was, in part, a response to the need for ordered leadership in the new church; and his ordination of Coke as a superintendent granted authority for superintending the work. Historically, elders have been set apart to order the church for its mission and service. The clergy members of the conference assumed responsibility for ordering in terms of recommending persons for ordination and maintaining the *Discipline.* The ordained ministry was responsible for the appointment and accountability of the ordained.

Much like sacramental authority, which is also granted to unordained persons, ordering was not solely related to ordination since unordained traveling preachers could be pastors in charge. Ordination, however, always included some aspect of ordering leadership within the church.

Itineracy

Though ordained persons could locate and lay preachers could also travel, ordination and itineracy have been closely related. Part of the covenant of ordination included the willingness to be itinerant. Itineracy was a function of conference membership, but was also related to one's ordination.

In summary, then, I believe that it is fair to say that, historically, Methodism's understanding of ordination has been primarily functional, even when some of those functions were also granted to non-ordained persons. The ordained were set apart for specific functions (including sacraments, preaching, and ordering or superintending) in service to the whole church and for the sake of the ministry of the whole people of God.

CHAPTER THREE

Toward New Understanding of Ordination

Yet for all the confusion and frustration that sometimes results, United Methodism has been remarkably effective in providing leadership for the churches. The new plan, like earlier ones, will have to be lived into over time by a tradition that prizes its pragmatism.
—Thomas Frank, *Polity, Practice and the Mission of The United Methodist Church*

The issues surrounding ordination call for thoughtful reflection by the whole Church. The historic understanding of ordination described in chapter 2 was radically revised by the 1996 General Conference, and the changes that are viewed as progress by some are considered unjustified departures from our heritage by others. William Lawrence notes that the 1996 General Conference "has sundered the relationship between ordination and the authorization to conduct the acts of ministry."[1] I would suggest that at least the potential for such a sundering exists at several points.

Implications of the 1996 Legislation

First, all probationary members (both deacon and elder candidates) will exercise their full ministry for three years without ordination, suggesting that ordination is not technically necessary for these functions. A particular concern exists regarding the administration of the sacraments; all probationary members serving as pastors will administer the sacraments for three years under a local pastor license. As in the past, probationary members will serve under the supervision of an elder, as do all local pastors. The significant change, however, is that in the past probationary members were ordained. It was their ordination as a deacon that granted them limited sacramental authority, thereby maintaining the connection between ordination and sacramental administration.

Before 1996 sacramental administration by unordained, licensed persons was the exception. Now it is the norm for all clergy during probation. In terms of granting authority for the functions of ministry, does licensing, commissioning, and election to probationary membership take precedence, thus making ordination superfluous? Or should the commissioned probationer on the elder track refrain from celebrating the sacraments and rely on an ordained elder, perhaps the district superintendent, for sacramental administration? Pragmatism notwithstanding, the direction of the current legislation continues to strain the historic tradition of Methodism and the Christian church regarding the link between ordination and sacrament.

Second, in regard to the deacon in full connection, there are no specific functions granted in ordination that cannot be carried out by laypersons by right of their baptism. Since there are no distinct functions reserved for the ordained deacon, we cannot continue to define ordination primarily in functional terms, as Methodism has usually done. What does ordination as a deacon mean functionally when many deacons will be carrying out the same tasks of ministry as diaconal ministers, missionaries, deaconesses, and other laypersons in specialized ministries in the Church? Also, what is the distinction between the ministry of a commissioned probationary member planning to be a deacon and the ministry of the deacon following ordination, or is ordination as a deacon unrelated to function? One clear implication is that since there are no functions of ministry authorized by ordination as a deacon that cannot be carried out by laity, a functional definition of ordination is no longer adequate for United Methodists.

Third, only elders are ordained to order. The primary meaning of ordination, to order, relates to the elders' responsibility for "ordering the Church for its mission and service, and administration of the *Discipline* of the Church" (¶ 303.2), which would include the responsibilities of district superintendents and bishops. Another significant ordering responsibility is election and supervision of the ordained. As full members of the annual conference, however, deacons in full connection will participate in all decisions about ordination and the discipline of clergy, even though they are not ordained to order; and lay members of the Board of Ordained Ministry will vote on issues of order, though not ordained at all. Lawrence writes, "Theologically, the question is not whether they should have such authorization. It is instead whether granting such 'ordering' authority to people not ordained to it undercuts the theological significance of ordination to 'order.' "[2]

If the focus of ordination, to order, is ordering the life and ministry of the Church and the administration of the *Discipline,* the ordination of the elder is quite distinct from that of the deacon, but at the point of ordering the life and practice of the ordained, the question Lawrence raises is worthy of consideration.

Fourth, elders will be ordained to service, but will not be ordained as deacon. This grants elders the same functions of ministry as the deacon without ordination as deacon. Potentially, this could undercut the distinct ministry and ordination of the deacon, but without it we run the risk of narrowing the ministry of the elder to that of a sacradotal parish priest while the deacon carries out servanthood in the world. This could, as Lawrence says, "further separate a servant ministry from a sacramental ministry."[3] But including service in the elder's ordination does have an impact on the creation of a distinct service ministry for the deacon.

Fifth, since service is now a function to which both deacons and elders are ordained, it is important to make clear how the ordination of deacons and elders to service differs from the call of all Christians to be in service/*diakonia*/ministry. Since all Christians are called to this ministry, ordination to service suggests no distinct function authorized by ordination that is not inherent in baptism.

71

These questions underscore the fact that under the new ordering of ministry, we no longer can assume a definition of ordination out of the Anglican tradition, as Wesley and Asbury did, nor can ordination be understood primarily in functional terms. Also, since we have created our own new pattern for ordained ministry, we can no longer assume an ecumenical definition or consistency with an ecumenical consensus. We must seek a new definition of United Methodist ordination that takes into account new forms of ordained ministry as envisioned in the 1996 General Conference legislation.

A Call for Prayerful Reflection by the Whole Church

A brief disciplinary paragraph created in a legislative process can never fully encompass the meaning of the sacred act of ordination and its place in the life of Christ's church. The Division of Ordained Ministry is planning a series of conversations during the 2001–2004 quadrennium that will bring together theologians, historians, ecumenical representatives, and lay and clergy leaders for careful study of this issue. Out of these conversations there likely will come future legislation so that the *Book of Discipline* can accurately reflect the understanding of the Church, but such legislation should grow out of thoughtful, prayerful consideration by the whole Church. As a contribution to that process I would suggest the following affirmations as basic steps toward a new understanding of ordination.

Ordination as God's gift to the church

In an incredible understatement, the disciplinary paragraph entitled "Purpose of Ordination" begins "Ordination to this ministry is a gift from God to the church." Rather than expand on what God does, the next sentence moves to ordination as an act of the church: "In ordination, the church affirms and continues the apostolic ministry through persons empowered by the Holy Spirit." Then the focus turns to what the ordinands do: "Those who are ordained make a commitment to conscious living of the whole gospel and to the proclamation of that gospel to the end that the world may be saved" (¶ 303).

Ordination as an act of God deserves more attention. Dennis Campbell stresses an understanding of ordination as God's act:

> The church is given leadership by God so that it can function in the world.
>
> The leadership God gives the church takes many different forms and involves a wide variety of people. . . . One form of leadership is that of ordained ministry, a gift from God to the church, and an act of God in the church. Putting it this way points to the fact that ordination is not just a human reality, in which the church, as a human community, establishes leadership; but it is God's reality in which the Holy Spirit empowers leadership for the sake of the Christian community.[4]

To understand ordination first as God's gift makes clear that it is more than an affirmation of the ordinand and his or her personal call. It is more than simply the church's authorization for ministry. It is not a matter of rights, privileges, or status. Rather, ordination is a matter of God's initiative for the sake of the whole church and the witness for Christ in the world.

Ordination as apostolic ministry

The ordained ministry of the church is rooted in the tradition of apostolic ministry, linking our current ministries with the ministry of the first apostles. David Bartlett, in his study of Luke's Gospel, points to the ascension narratives where Jesus "passes that kerygma on to the apostles (who in turn pass it to Paul and through Paul to Luke's own church). At the ascension, Jesus says to the eleven: 'But you will receive power when the Holy Spirit has come upon you; and you will be my witnesses in Jerusalem, in all Judea and Samaria, and to the ends of the earth' (Acts 1:8). The apostles, therefore, became both the heirs and the guarantors of Jesus' ministry."[5] Bartlett acknowledges that the office of apostle ceases with the ministry of the twelve, but "what remains, however, is the apostolic ministry—or ministry in continuity with the apostles. Such ministry includes teaching, healing, and above all the kerygma."[6]

Though we as United Methodists would not claim apostolic ordination as an unbroken line linking us directly with the first apostles in apostolic succession, we would affirm ordination as the continuation of the apostolic task, the teaching and proclaiming ministry of those who have been set apart in order to ensure faithful transmission of the gospel from generation to generation and to assure the church of appropriate leadership. The *Discipline* affirms this connection in the first paragraphs of the section entitled "The Ministry of the Ordained": "Ministry in the Christian church is derived from the ministry of Christ. . . . Within the church community, there are persons whose gifts, evidence of God's grace, and promise of future usefulness are affirmed by the community, and who respond to God's call by offering themselves in leadership as ordained ministers" (¶ 301).

Paragraph 302 then describes ordination and apostolic ministry:

> The pattern for this response to the call is provided in the development of the early church. The apostles led in prayer and preaching, ordered the spiritual and temporal life of the community, established leadership for the ministry of service, and provided for the proclamation of the gospel to new persons and in new places. The early church, through the laying on of hands, set apart persons with responsibility to preach, to teach, to administer the sacraments, to nurture, to heal, to gather the community in worship, and to send them forth in witness. The church also set apart other persons to care for the physical needs of others, reflecting the concerns for the people of the world. In the New Testament (Acts 6), we see the apostles identifying and authorizing persons to a ministry of service. These functions, though set apart, were never separate from the ministry of the whole people of God. Paul states (Ephesians 4:1-12) that different gifts and ministries are given to all persons.

In describing the purpose of ordination, ¶ 303 goes on to say that "the church affirms and continues the apostolic ministry through persons empowered by the Holy Spirit" and concludes with the awesome challenge for ordinands to make "a commitment to conscious living of the whole gospel and to the proclamation of that gospel to the end that the world may be saved." For elders, the apostolic task is clearly stated in their responsibility for "preaching and teaching the word of God, [and the] administration of the sacraments." For deacons, the *Discipline* is not as clear, but I would suggest that the only way to understand their ordination to Word is as ordination to the apostolic task.

Ordained apostolic leaders are essential to the ongoing vitality of the Church and its faithful witness in the world. The *Discipline* offers a fitting climax to the affirmation of apostolic ministry when it says, "The effectiveness of the Church in mission depends on these covenantal commitments to the ministry of all Christians and the ordained ministry of the Church. Through ordination and through other offices of pastoral leadership, the Church provides for the continuation of Christ's ministry, which has been committed to the church as a whole" (¶ 303.4).

Ordination as calling

In keeping with the Wesleyan emphasis on the call, ordination represents the outward call of the Church, affirming the inward call of the individual responding in faith to God's initiative. "Those whom the Church ordains shall be conscious of God's call to ordained ministry, and their call shall be acknowledged and authenticated by the Church" (¶ 301.1). The section of the *Discipline* entitled "Wesley's Questions for Examiners" says that the purpose for examination is "that The United Methodist Church may be assured that those persons who present themselves as candidates for ministry are truly called of God to this order" (¶ 305). The experience of God's call in the lives of individual candidates and the Church's confirmation of that call distinguish the ministry of the ordained from the ministry of all baptized Christians.

Ordination as identity

If we can no longer define ordination in primarily functional terms, we can say that ordination grants a new identity. The individual becomes an ordained representative of the Church, set apart and sent in the name of the Christ and the Church with an identity distinct within the whole people of God. Frederick Buechner's poetic paragraph describes it well:

> You will be ordained ... and if your experience is anything like mine, you will find that something more even than an outlandish new title and an outlandish new set of responsibilities is conferred in that outlandish ceremony. Without wanting to sound unduly fanciful, I think it is fair to say that an extraordinary new adventure begins with ordination, a new stretch of the road, that is unlike any other that you have either experienced or imagined. Your life is no longer your own in the same sense. You are not anymore virtuous than you ever were—certainly no new sanctity or wisdom or power suddenly descends—but you are nonetheless "on call" in a new way. You start moving through the world as the declared representative of what people variously see as either the world's oldest and most persistent and superannuated superstition, or the world's wildest and most improbably dream, or the holy living truth itself.[7]

It may sound redundant, but to be ordained is to become an ordained minister. Ordination brings a new identity. When commissioned ministers who have been serving as pastors under a local pastor license become ordained elders, they will continue in the same function of ministry but will have a new identity. When diaconal ministers are ordained as deacons in full connection, many will continue to do the same functions of ministry they did before; but they will carry a new identity in the Church and in the world, no longer as laity, but appointed and sent by the bishop as ordained representatives of the Church.

Ordination as leadership in ministry

The *Discipline* makes clear that part of the purpose of ordination is to set apart leadership to enable the ministry of the whole Church.

> Within the church community, there are persons whose gifts, evidence of God's grace, and promise of future usefulness are

affirmed by the community, and who respond to God's call by offering themselves in leadership as ordained ministers. (¶ 301.2)

Ordination is fulfilled in leadership of the people of God through ministries of Service, Word, Sacrament, and Order. . . . Those who respond to God's call to lead in service and to equip others for this ministry through teaching, proclamation, and worship and who assist elders in the administration of the sacraments are ordained deacons. Those whose leadership in service includes preaching and teaching the Word of God, administration of the sacraments, ordering the Church for its mission and service, and administration of the *Discipline* of the Church are ordained as elders. (¶ 303.2)

This concise statement outlines the role of the ordained within the whole Church and in relation to the ministry of all of the baptized.

Leadership in ministry assumes authority and responsibility for equipping the whole Church for ministry in the world for the sake of Christ. Ordained persons are set apart distinctly for this leadership role. The *Discipline* says, "The privilege of servant leadership in the Church is the call to share in the preparation of congregations and the whole Church for the mission of God in the world" (¶ 315).

Ordination as membership in the Orders

Here I use the word *order* in the sense of the Order of Deacons and the Order of Elders (¶¶ 310-14), not in relationship to the elder's ordination to order the ministry of the Church. New to the 1996 *Book of Discipline* is the call for Orders, covenant communities that will "provide for . . . continuing formation in relationship to Jesus Christ . . . develop a bond of unity and common commitment to the mission and ministry of The United Methodist Church and the annual conference . . . [and] enable the creation of relationships that allow mutual support and trust" (¶ 312). Only ordained deacons and elders will be members of their respective Orders, since it is by ordination that one becomes a member of the Order.

The provisional ordinal says, "Ordination is a gift from God to the church and is exercised in covenant with the whole church, and within the covenant of the Order and includes specific vows concerning the ordinands' willingness to participate in this covenant community. The candidate is asked 'Will you covenant to participate in the Order of Deacons/Elders? Will you give yourself to God through the Order of Deacons/Elders in order to sustain and build each other up in prayer, study, worship and service?' "[8]

The creation of Orders has the potential of recovering the function of the early conferences in Methodism when the traveling preachers came together for discipline, fraternity and revival.[9] In fact, Russell Richey uses the word *order* when he describes Wesley's conference as "a family of preachers . . . a monastic-like order held together by affection, by common rules, by a shared mission and by watchfulness of each member over one another; it functioned as a brotherhood of religious aspiration and song."[10] Though we have no intent of literally following the model implied here as it relates to gender, it helps to view the new Orders in light of this history. The creation of Orders seeks to recover in a new way for a new day this sense of common covenant and mutual caring among those whose life and work are bound together in conference membership and ordination.

One of the clear distinctions, then, between lay ministry and ordained ministry will be commitment to and participation in the disciplined life of a covenant community of which one becomes a member by ordination for the sake of the whole Church.

Ordination and accountability

Though for United Methodist clergy this aspect of ordination is closely related to conference membership, an ordinand accepts accountability to the covenant community and "the authority of the bishop and others appointed to supervise your ministry"[11] as an integral part of ordination. One of the most eloquent paragraphs in the *Book of Discipline* defines the nature of the clergy covenant:

Elders in full connection with an annual conference by virtue of their election and ordination are bound in special covenant with all the ordained elders of the annual conference. In the keeping of this covenant they perform the ministerial duties and maintain the ministerial standards established by those in the covenant. They offer themselves without reserve to be appointed and to serve, after consultation, as the appointive authority may determine. They live with all other ordained ministers in mutual trust and concern and seek with them the sanctification of the fellowship. By entering into the covenant, they accept and subject themselves to the process of clergy discipline. (¶ 324)

In the qualifications for ordination outlined at the beginning of candidacy, one of the expectations is that candidates will "be accountable to The United Methodist Church, accept its *Discipline* and authority, accept the supervision of those appointed to this ministry, and be prepared to live in the covenant of its ordained ministers" (¶ 304.1*i*). To be ordained is to be accountable to the Church and to other members of the Order for one's life and ministry. It means that my only authority to perform the rites of the Church resides in the community and that my accountability is not just to myself, but to the *Discipline* of the conference and to my brothers and sisters in the clergy session.

Conclusion

We will look more closely at the distinct ordination of deacons and elders in chapters 6 and 7. Our purpose here is to seek foundational affirmations for a new understanding of ordination in United Methodism that comprehends two distinct Orders, is congruent with our roots, and gives meaning to the act as it relates to the ministry of all Christians. At this point, therefore, I would suggest beginning by considering ordination as God's gift of apostolic leadership through those who are called to a new identity on behalf of the Church to live and serve in an ordered life, accountable to one another and to the whole Church for their life and ministry.

CHAPTER FOUR

Commissioning and Ordaining

The act of commissioning probationary members
* *Acknowledges and affirms God's call and the candidates' response, gifts, abilities and training for servant leadership*
* *Invokes God's grace for true service*
* *Credentials candidates to lead the church and equip others for ministry*
* *Calls candidates to enter a time of evaluation;*
* *Offers candidates the support of the annual conference*
                    —*Revised Services for the Ordering of Ministry*
                              in The United Methodist Church

The 1996 ministry legislation created commissioning as a new liturgical act to mark persons entering probationary membership. Commissioning has been used previously in a variety of ways in the life of the Church, including the commissioning of lay workers, missionaries, deaconesses, and mission work teams. This is the first time, however, that it has been used in relation to ordination and conference membership. This decision by the General Conference, therefore, created a new form of the ordered ministry and a liturgical act that has no precedence in our history or ecumenical consensus. It is one of the new creations of our 1996 ordering of ministry. As a starting point, it is helpful to understand how it came about.

Background

Prior to 1996 persons were received into probationary membership and ordained deacon, usually in the same session of the annual conference. Reception into probationary membership established a relationship with the conference, and ordination authorized deacons to carry out the functions of ordination (Word, Sacrament, and Order) in a limited way during probation. The proposal that came to the 1996 General Conference from the Council of Bishops called for a continuation of this practice, with two significant changes: First, ordination as a deacon would be clearly defined as ordination to servant ministry in the world; and second, some deacons would continue in ministries of service for a lifetime and be received into full membership in the annual conference as "deacons in full connection." Deacons who were called to ministries of Word, Sacrament, and Order would subsequently be ordained elder and received into full membership.[1]

The first and major change the General Conference legislative committee made to this recommendation from the bishops was to create a separate ordination for deacons in full connection and call for the direct ordination of elders, both following probation. This meant that probationary members would no longer be ordained. At that point the legislative committee struggled with two questions: If probationary members are not ordained, what liturgical act will recognize this step in ministry; and since probationary membership carries no authority for the functions of ministry, how will those who serve as pastors be authorized for their ministry?

After much discussion the legislative committee recommended a two-part solution to these questions. First, commissioning would become the new liturgical act marking entrance into probationary membership; and second, a local pastor license would be used to grant probationers serving as pastors the authority for pastoral ministry, including sacramental administration, under the disciplinary principle that "all persons not ordained as elders who are appointed to preach and conduct divine worship and perform the duties of a pastor shall have a license as a local pastor" (¶ 341).

Probationary members preparing for ordination as deacon would not need such a license since they would not be serving as pastors in charge and there are no specific functions thus restricted to the deacon in full connection.

In a swift act of linguistic creativity, the legislative committee replaced the term "ordination as a deacon" in what was to become ¶ 316 with the word *commissioning,* so that a paragraph that was written to define a form of ordination, now defines an act that was intended *not* to be ordination.

These recommendations went to the General Conference plenary and were approved with little discussion or debate.

Distinction Between Commissioning and Ordination

Thus far the best attempt to create a distinction between commissioning and ordination is the work of the Ordinal Revision Working Group.[2] It reflects thoughtful work by representatives of the General Board of Higher Education and Ministry, the Board of Discipleship, and the Council of Bishops and was the foundation for the new definition of commissioning that was adopted by the 2000 General Conference, as outlined in appendix 6. The provisional *Revised Services* have been used in every annual conference; and detailed feedback from the conferences, the Council of Bishops, lay leaders, and theologians has been considered and incorporated. The pertinent section of that document appears in appendix 1. The working group interprets commissioning in the following ways.

Commissioning is temporary and ordination is for lifetime service.

"One aspect distinguishing the commissioning of probationary members from ordination of elders and deacons is duration: *Commissioning* sends persons to a term of service, while *ordination* sets persons apart for lifelong service" (italics added).[3] The working group understood commissioning to be specifically related to the time of probationary membership that comes to an end "when the person is received as a full member of the annual conference and ordained a deacon or elder, or a decision is made not to proceed toward ordination."[4] Commissioning has duration (normally three years) and carries no lasting meaning in regard to the set-apart ministry of the Church; whereas ordination is for a lifetime, and therefore, once persons are ordained, they would not be reordained in the future.

Commissioning represents the initial sending of persons in service, while ordination represents identity and authority as an ordained representative of the Church.

The working group reviewed the use of the word *commissioning* in other places in the Church and discovered that it always carries with it a sense of sending. Therefore, they concluded, "Commissioning implies that the person is being 'sent' by the annual conference for service and the annual conference invokes the Holy Spirit to empower commissioned ministers during this time of probationary membership." On the other hand, ordination "has to do with who the person *is* as well as what the person *does* in ministry" (italics added).[5] Ordination grants a new identity and an authority for the functions of ministry not included or implied in commissioning. The provisional ordinal and the *Book of Discipline* clearly state that commissioning carries no authority for the functions of ministry beyond proclaiming and equipping. Otherwise ordination becomes superfluous.[6]

Commissioning marks a step in a journey toward ordination.

Ordination is the completion of a journey of formation including education, mentoring, and training that begins with the call, proceeds through candidacy and probationary membership, and culminates in ordination and full conference membership. "The rite of ordination is the climax of a process in which the faith community discerns and validates the call, the gifts, and effectiveness for apostolic ministry by agency of the Holy Spirit."[7] Commissioning marks a particular point along that journey—the step of probationary membership in the conference—but does not carry the sense of fulfillment that is part of ordination.

Ordination is a gift of God and commissioning is an act of the church.

At this point I would move beyond the working group and propose another possible distinction. Though it is subject to question, I would at least raise it for consideration as one possible way to discuss the focus of these two acts: One is focused on God's action; the other, on the church—though both acts include God and the church.

Paragraph 316 begins, "Commissioning is the act of the Church," whereas ¶ 303 says, "Ordination to this ministry is a gift from God to the church." I don't want to make too much of this language since, as we have already seen, one can legitimately question whether the legislative committee or the General Conference gave enough thought to it, but it might be helpful to think about these actions as having two different foci. Undoubtedly, God is involved in both acts, as is the Church; but the focus of commissioning is on the action of the Church in acknowledging God's call and the gifts of the candidates and on inviting the Holy Spirit to empower candidates for ministry. The focus of ordination is on God's activity in the lives of the ordinands and in the community in setting persons apart for a lifetime of leadership. As we try to give meaning to the legislation passed by the 1996 General Conference and clarify these two separate actions, perhaps this interpretation will help.

The Laying on of Hands

The first record of the laying on of hands in the Christian church is probably the account in Acts 13:1-3 where Barnabas and Saul were set apart and sent in mission. Laying on of hands with prayer by the bishop continues to represent the continuity of ordination through the past, in the present, and into the future. It is the mark of setting apart for leadership in the church by ordination. For United Methodists, however, laying on of hands is also used in baptism, confirmation, commissioning of missionaries and deaconesses, and consecration of diaconal ministers and bishops. In each setting the prayer interprets the meaning of the act. Mary Elizabeth Moore suggested to the working group: "This issue seems to have taken on more significance than is proportional in the light of the history of the church, particularly The United Methodist Church."[8] Though she may be correct, it is not an issue of small concern since it is an important link with the entire history and pattern of Christian ministry.

The Laying on of Hands in Ordination

The text of the provisional ordinal emphasizes the role of the bishop as the presiding officer of the annual conference and as a general superintendent for the whole Church who in the laying on of hands represents the whole Church (both laity and clergy) and serves as the link with the apostolic ministry through the centuries. "The connection through the physical touch between the ordinand and those who participate in the laying on of hands establishes the real connection between those who share in ordained ministry and symbolically connects the ordinand to all those who have shared in this ministry . . . in all ages."[9] To signify this connection and to represent the Orders into which persons are ordained, the recommendation is that "the bishop, as the presiding officer of the annual conference and general superintendent leads deacons in laying hands on those who are to be ordained deacon in full connection and leads the elders in laying hands on those who are to be ordained elders."[10]

The 1996 *Book of Discipline* follows the pattern established in 1988, which grants bishops the authority to decide if persons who do not share the Order into which the candidate is being ordained should participate in the laying on of hands. Presumably, this could include elders laying hands on deacons, deacons laying hands on elders, ecumenical guests joining in the laying on of hands, or laity laying hands on deacons or elders (¶¶ 321.5, 324). Unfortunately, inclusion of laity in the laying on of hands has become a volatile political issue related to the empowerment of laypersons, reminiscent of the Methodist Protestant movement. In the process, the important and necessary desire to affirm lay ministry can become confused with the sacred act of setting apart leaders and their entrance into a covenant community of those called to lead and to serve the whole Church through ordination. The fact that laity and clergy alike have used and abused the tradition and have failed to fully understand its symbolism contributes to the confusion. It is probably fair to say that throughout the Church there is little understanding of the meaning of the act or its place in church tradition. The fact that we have also neglected a proper emphasis on the ministry of all Christians opens the way for the current debate.

The provision for laity to participate in the laying on of hands is a recent change, enacted in 1988. At this point the legislative history of this departure from the tradition of Methodism and of most branches of the Christian church is insightful. Prior to 1988 there was no reference to lay participation in the laying on of hands. United Methodists and all our antecedent bodies maintained the principle that responsibility for ordination rests in the community of the ordained, that the ministry ordains the ministry. This had been reaffirmed as recently as 1980 in the publication of the alternative ordinal, which clearly specified ordination by the bishop and other elders because "the meaning of that symbol is clear only when those who participate in that 'symbolic act' also share the same representative ministry of pastoral office being conferred. The meaning of that symbol is distorted, and the distinction between general and ordained ministry is blurred, when unordained persons are invited to join in the laying on of hands."[11]

Then, only eight years later, language to include laity designated by the bishop was recommended by the legislative committee and approved by the General Conference on the consent calendar, meaning without any discussion or debate by the conference. Ever since then there has been extensive discussion, particularly among the Council of Bishops and conference lay leaders. In 1997 the council adopted a statement that basically gives each bishop the freedom to decide who to include in the act. The text of the statement is in appendix 4.

David Tripp provides a thorough history and analysis of the issue in his recent article "Ordination: Laying on of Hands and the

Role of the Laity," in the journal *Doxology.* He details the development of the symbol from Acts 13 to the present and concludes that it is the prayer that, in fact, is the core of ordination, with the whole community joining in that prayer. He says, "The laying on of hands . . . is secondary, even if integral, to the ordination prayer."[12] Since the prayer includes the whole community and the bishop represents the whole Church, the Ordinal Revision Working Group rightly questioned why anyone else should take part except the bishop.

Tripp suggests that a more appropriate form of lay participation would be "the tradition of the instruments, *porrectio instrumentorum,* the handing over of the tools for the job."[13] He argues that if a layperson were to deliver the Bible to the ordinand, it would be "highly visible. . . . It would not submerge a lay representative in a shoal of clerical persons, and make such an inserted person look like an afterthought."[14] He draws our attention to the fact that the new *Methodist Worship Book* of the British Methodist Church gives this duty to the vice president of the conference, who is always a layperson.

The provisional *Revised Services* begins with a powerful witness to the ministry of all Christians in a "Recognition of Our Common Ministry," affirming baptism as the foundation of all ministry. All ordinands come from the ranks of the laity and have been approved by the pastor-parish relations committee, the charge conference, the district committee, and the conference board of ordained ministry, all of which include laity. It is therefore most appropriate for laypersons to participate in the ordination service in the "Recognition of Our Common Ministry" and in the presentation of candidates, symbolic of ordained ministry rooted in the ministry of the baptized. Laity should be visible, active participants in the service of ordination, particularly at this point representing the unity of ministry and baptism as the basis for ordination.

In the laying on of hands, the bishop, as general superintendent, represents the whole Church, including laity and clergy, with clergy members representing the Order into which persons are being ordained. Since the ministry of all Christians has already been affirmed as the context of the act of ordaining, lay participation at this point seems redundant and confuses the symbolism of setting apart for an ordered ministry. With the new emphasis on ordination into the Order of Deacons and Order of Elders, it seems most appropriate to focus on the particular Order into which the person is being ordained, symbolized by representatives of that Order joining the bishop in the laying on of hands.

Ecumenical participation in various aspects of the service, particularly by representatives of the Consultation on Church Union (COCU; Church of Christ Uniting), is encouraged as a symbol of ordained ministry as one form within the universal ministry of the church of Jesus Christ and of the ecumenical commitments of United Methodism. If ecumenical representatives take part in the laying on of hands, they should be "bishops of other traditions and ecumenical representatives with ordaining authority."[15] Here again, it might be best for ecumenical representatives to participate at places other than the laying on of hands since United Methodism has defined ordination in a way that is not altogether shared by other denominations.

In summary, the recommendations of the working group conclude, "The whole church is present in the prayer of the presiding bishop. Whatever purposes the participation of others in the laying on of hands may serve, it cannot be that they would otherwise not participate in the ordination. For this reason, configurations that aim to include elders, deacons, non-ordained persons, and ecumenical guests in an attempt to achieve comprehensive, representative participation in the laying on of hands are particularly to be avoided."[16]

The ongoing reflection about the meaning of the laying on of hands by the working group, the Council of Bishops, ecumenical groups, lay leadership, and the whole Church will be essential to the future of ordained ministry in United Methodism. Our theologians, historians, and liturgical experts need to help us to think through our practice in light of Scripture, tradition, reason, and experience and to create liturgies that are consistent with Christian tradition and clearly express our new understanding of ministry, which includes the ministry of all Christians and two Orders of ordained ministry.

Laying on of hands in commissioning

The phrase "laying on of hands" was included in the paragraph defining commissioning because the paragraph was originally written to define a form of ordination. The General Conference legislative committee and plenary did not discuss the implications of using the laying on of hands in both acts; but since laying on of hands is used in a variety of liturgies including baptism, confirmation, the commissioning of deaconesses and missionaries, and the consecration of bishops, it is not inappropriate to use it here. It is important, however, to make clear the distinction between commissioning and ordination since the General Conference specifically rejected the bishops' proposal for ordination at the point of probationary membership and in its place created the liturgical act of commissioning.

To try to make a distinction between the act in these two liturgies, the working group recommends that commissioning take place at a time other than ordination. Since commissioning does not represent entrance into an Order, it would seem to be most appropriate for laity to participate in the laying on of hands in commissioning rather than in ordination since this act clearly marks the step from the ranks of the laity to identification as a clergyperson. Commissioned members are members of the clergy and no longer laity, so this marks the point of transition. The working group says, "This act is clearly connected to the ministry of all Christians from which commissioned ministers come and within which they serve. Commissioning fits well within 'An Annual Conference Service for the Celebration of Christ's Ministry.' "[17]

If the two liturgies are included in one service, a possible alternative is for the bishop to extend hands over the group of candidates to be commissioned or to lay hands on the shoulder instead of on the head. But ultimately the text of the liturgy must define the purpose of the laying on of hands in ordination and commissioning.

Ecumenical Implications

Without a doubt, it is at this point of creating the new liturgical act called commissioning that United Methodism has taken the biggest step away from our historic practice and from ecumenical consensus by creating an entirely new office and form of ministry. The ecumenical question yet to be answered is how this new, uniquely United Methodist commissioned minister will relate to the orders of other denominations. The notion of non-ordained clergy is an oxymoron in some traditions. Our use of non-ordained local pastors to extend the sacramental ministry of the ordained elder has always raised questions with Roman Catholic, Anglican, and Orthodox traditions, but we have explained this practice as our pragmatic missional exception. Now pastoral leadership including sacramental administration by non-ordained, commissioned clergy will be the standard practice during probation. How we interpret commissioning within the ecumenical community as we seek mutual recognition with other COCU denominations, our sister Methodist denominations, and other Christian churches will be important to our ecumenical relations as well as to our self-understanding. If mutual recognition of orders is to have any integrity, we must meet the demand that we be clear about the forms of ministry we have created and openly acknowledge our uniquely United Methodist ordering of ministry, even if it means straining our ecumenical dialogue.

Conclusion

This significant change calls for careful interpretation of our practice. If the act of commissioning is given too much weight, it could inadvertently weaken the power of ordination, making it seem redundant. On the other hand, because commissioned ministers will have completed their educational requirements and most will be serving as pastors in charge of local congregations, the act must have an appropriate depth of meaning and power. How the Church balances these concerns will be important if we are to give commissioning significant meaning without under-mining ordination.

The creation of the liturgical act of commissioning may well prove to be one of the most helpful and creative acts of the 1996 ministry legislation, or it may be the most confusing and misun-derstood aspect of our new ordering of ministry. If we are to seek the former and avoid the latter, we must work to interpret clear-ly the distinct meanings of ordination and commissioning so that our liturgy truly reflects our theology and polity and the setting apart of ordained leaders continues to be significant in the life of the Church.

CHAPTER FIVE

Servant Ministry, Representative Ministry, and Apostolic Ministry

Within The United Methodist Church, there are those called to servant leadership, lay and ordained. . . . The privilege of servant leadership in the Church is the call to share in the preparation of congregations and the whole Church for the mission of God in the world. The obligation of servant leadership is the forming of Christian disciples in the covenant community of the congregation.
—The Book of Discipline, ¶ 115

The 1996 *Discipline* replaced the short-lived term "representative ministry" with the terms "servant ministry" and "servant leadership." This change has wide-ranging implications since it occupies an important place in the paragraphs dealing with the mission and ministry of the Church and serves as an introduction to the section on the ministry of the ordained (¶¶ 301-365). In addition, the term "apostolic ministry" is used in paragraphs ¶¶ 302 and 303. These terms are basic to our understanding of ordination and how we speak of the various forms of ministry in the Church.

Representative Ministry

The terms "general ministry" and "representative ministry" were introduced in 1976 in the report of the Ministry Study Commission to General Conference in an attempt to define general ministry (i.e., the ministry of all Christians) and ordained ministry, "showing thereby their inherent relationship and interdependence, yet at the same time delineating their distinctiveness."[1] The phrase "representative ministry" was meant to include the two forms of professional ministry, the consecrated diaconal minister and the ordained deacon and elder, as distinct from the general ministry of all Christians.

In many ways the term "representative ministry" was helpful in speaking of persons set apart for specialized ministries by ordination and consecration. Though it was never clearly defined in the text, at its best it had the potential, according to William Lawrence, to identify ordained and consecrated ministries as "representing the church to God (in liturgy, prayer, and pastoral presence); representing Christ to the church (in presiding at the Table, in a model as servant); and representing Christ to the world (in witness, service, love, and sacrifice)."[2] This concept figured centrally in the 1982 World Council of Churches document *Baptism, Eucharist and Ministry* as well as in COCU consensus documents.[3]

Richard Heitzenrater notes, however, "There is some problem knowing just what representative means: it seems to mean everything and therefore nothing. The special ministry is representative of Christ(!), of the whole church, of the entire community of Christ, of the Gospel; special ministry represents to the church its identity with Christ and the Gospel itself."[4]

For twenty years the term was both bane and blessing, offering both clarity and confusion until 1996 when the Council of Bishops' report to the 1996 General Conference recommended that the terms "servant ministry" and "servant leadership" replace "representative ministry" in the *Discipline*. This change was adopted by the General Conference, but has created its own confusion.

Servant Ministry and Servant Leadership

These terms reflect a theme that undergirds the new ordering of ministry: an emphasis on service (*diakonia*) rooted in baptism as a basic element of all ministry. The *Book of Discipline* assumes that "the Church's ministry of service is *a primary representation* of God's love" (¶ 303.2), and in ¶ 310 service is not just *a* primary representation, but "*the* primary form of [Jesus Christ's] ministry in God's name" (italics added).

Given this basic assumption, servant leadership has the potential of defining a style of leadership, a call for both lay and clergy leaders to pattern their ministry after the Servant Christ, who came to serve, not to be served, in contrast to a style that derives from notions of privilege, status, and power. Though well intended, use of the term could, on the other hand, contribute to a weakening of the authority of ordained ministry if there is no clear understanding of the leadership role as well as the servant heart of ordained clergy in the Church.

The term "servant leadership," like its predecessor "representative ministry," is never clearly defined. As Thomas Frank notes, "First, it is not a phrase particular to ecclesiology; it has been widely used in recent years in American management literature as a name for an ideal executive role in all kinds of organizations. . . . Secondly, the term is not specifically connected with the church's historic manner of ordering its communal life, namely the language of offices."[5]

Another sensitive concern relates to the connotation of the word *servant* for persons who have frequently found themselves in subservient roles, particularly ethnic minorities and women. Without careful explanation, this language can carry negative connotations for persons who have been treated as second-class citizens and often relegated to the role of servant. Likewise, deacons, who all too often have been seen in the second-class role of a servant, may question whether this language is helpful in affirming their ministry alongside the ministry of the elders. Finally, for powerful white male clergy who assume the authority of their position, the use of this language can promote a false modesty that denies their significant place and role in leadership and keeps them from dealing with issues of power and identity.

These concerns are worthy of careful reflection and suggest that we should not uncritically adopt such significant language without full reflection on its potential for good and for confusion. In this regard, the first step is to acknowledge the vast difference between those who have been oppressed or forced into service and those who have chosen the lifestyle of servanthood as an act of free will in response to Christ's call. Jesus says the servant will, in fact, be first in the great reversal of roles and values that takes place in the reign of God: "Whoever wishes to become great among you must be your servant, and whoever wishes to be first among you must be slave of all" (Mark 10:43-44).

Another problem arises from the fact that this term refers to both ordained and lay leadership and therefore fails to distinguish between them since a paragraph that used to identify those set apart by consecration and ordination now, in effect, refers to all lay and ordained ministry. The result is that the term "servant leadership" does not define the set-apart ministry, but tends to be just another way of speaking of the ministry of all Christians. In this sense the term is helpful in describing a style of ministry that should be evident in the ministry of all Christians; but given its location in the *Discipline,* it fails to provide the needed distinction between ordained ministry and the ministry of all Christians.

The result, according to Thomas Frank, is "language that as it stands will surely increase the ambivalence and lack of clarity in United Methodism about the respective role of lay and ordained ministry. . . . What exactly is special about the 'specialized ministries' of the ordained remains ambiguous and largely undefined."[6]

William Lawrence suggests another weakness of the term "servant leadership":

> While the phrase may look unobjectionable, it lacks the richness and subtle nuance of the now absent "representative ministry." For one thing, "servant leadership" does not adequately express the transcendent aspects of representing the people to God or Christ to the people and to the world. Rather, it is limited to the perspective of immanence: the human Jesus, the despised suffering servant, or the successful business or political leader. This is democratization, or leveling, of theology that risks robbing our doctrine of its mystery, and hence of its power.[7]

Apostolic Ministry

At a time when the Church is calling for visionary, responsible leadership, a time that calls for clear articulation of the gospel and faithful transmission of the Word to a biblically illiterate generation, a recovery of the historic concept of apostolic ministry could strengthen ordained ministry, address the confusion of servant language, and reclaim the best of representative ministry.

The phrase "apostolic ministry" seems in many ways dated and out of touch. Few United Methodist clergy are familiar with it, and my guess is that most United Methodists would barely recognize it. However, it has a rich history and still appears in the title of ¶ 302 and in the text of ¶ 303, "The Purpose of Ordination," which says, "In ordination, the church affirms and continues the apostolic ministry through persons empowered by the Holy Spirit."

In an excellent article entitled "The Apostolic Character of Ordained Ministry,"[8] Robert Neville bases an understanding of apostolic ministry on 1 Corinthians 15, where Paul describes his own ministry, a model of what the church has associated with ordination. Neville suggests that the language of apostolic ministry points to a reality beyond the immediate human context and affirms God's historic presence in and through ordained ministry in the church, whereas representative and servant language seems to grow out of the immediate context for ministry. Paul clearly states that it is "by the grace of God I am what I am, and his grace toward me has not been in vain" (1 Cor 15:10), and in that sense the term "apostolic ministry" picks up the notion of persons called by God and set apart in the tradition of the first apostles.

Neville also lifts up apostolic ministry, not as a career, but as a calling. It is not a "career option . . . but rather has to do with the need of God to find vehicles to effect the redemption of the world."[9] It is a task one does not choose, but accepts. The acceptance of this call brings about a change in one's identity and self-understanding. Whereas all Christians are called to represent Christ in the world in witness and ministry, and all Christians by their baptism are called to servanthood, the ordained person takes on a particular identity in the church for the sake of the church's ministry in the world in response to God's gracious call.

This new identity includes responsibility for leadership within the body of Christ. The ministry of leadership must always be exercised with the heart of a servant, but it is clearly leadership. Neville says, "Apostolic leadership consists in leadership that is responsible to the whole of the Christian mission. . . . Service is effective responsiveness to a need . . . leadership involves a readiness to tell people what they don't want to hear and to get them to do things they don't want to do."[10]

Finally, Neville stresses that "for apostolic ministry, the gospel is first and foremost to be preached."[11] Paul states the central *kerygma,* the message of "first importance . . . that Christ died for our sins in accordance with the scriptures, and that he was buried, and that he was raised on the third day in accordance with the scriptures, and that he appeared to Cephas, then to the twelve" (1 Cor 15:3-5).

The new ordering of ministry affirms the apostolic ministry of the Word as central for both the deacon and the elder. Although the elder has the primary responsibility for the preaching ministry, deacons are also ordained to proclaim the Word. This central commitment to make known God's Word is essential to ordained ministry. To emphasize servanthood at the expense of the apostolic role has the potential of minimizing the evangelistic, prophetic task, unless ordination to Service is rooted in ordination to Word. Without the primacy of the Word, service by the church cannot be distinguished from service by many worthy and valuable civic, social, and governmental programs responding to human need. The civic and business club Rotary, for example, has as its motto "Service Above Self" and carries out extensive service projects around the world. The cup of cold water, however, remains only water unless it is given in the name of Jesus. Apostolic ministry proclaims the Word, which is acted out in the deed. It is the apostolic identity, the calling to the faithful communication of God's Word made flesh in Jesus Christ that gives the church's service its distinct flavor and provides the unique identity of those set apart by ordination for leadership.

Conclusion

Those who are ordained share with all Christians the task of representing Christ to the world and of servant ministry, *diakonia*. Their unique calling is expressed in being set apart for the apostolic ministry of proclaiming the Word and leading and equipping all Christians for witness and service. They carry the name and identity of Christ's people in a unique way, and as apostolic ministers they accept the task of the faithful transmission of the faith and the proclamation of the Word from generation to generation.

From the days of the first apostles until today, the church has relied on persons set apart for the apostolic task of teaching and proclaiming the faith and leading the church in mission. These persons are set apart by God and by the community within the context of the community, not for their own sake, but for the sake of the gospel, to ensure that the community is grounded in Scripture, rooted in its faith tradition, and propelled in service in the world.

The 1996 *Book of Discipline* clearly states, "Ordained persons exercise their ministry in covenant with all Christians, especially with those whom they lead and serve in ministry. . . . The effectiveness of the Church in mission depends on these covenantal commitments to the ministry of all Christians and to the ordained ministry of the Church. Through ordination and through other offices of pastoral leadership, the Church provides for the continuation of Christ's ministry, which has been committed to the church as a whole. Without the creative use of the diverse gifts of the entire body of Christ, the ministry of the Church is less effective. Without responsible leadership, the focus, direction and continuity of that ministry is diminished" (¶ 303.3-4).

This is the calling and the task of the ordained: apostolic leadership within the context of the representative, servant ministry of the whole people of God.

CHAPTER SIX

The Traveling Elder in Full Connection

Elders are ordained to a lifetime ministry of Service, Word, Sacrament and Order. They are authorized to preach and teach the Word of God, to administer the sacraments of baptism and Holy Communion, and to order the life of the Church for mission and ministry. The servant leadership of the elder is expressed by leading the people of God in worship and prayer, by leading persons to faith in Jesus Christ, by exercising pastoral supervision in the congregation, and by leading the Church in obedience to mission in the world.

As members of the Order of Elder, all elders are in covenant with all other elders in the annual conference and shall participate in the life of their Order.

—*The Book of Discipline,* ¶ 323

This brief but powerful statement succinctly captures the scope of the ministry of the United Methodist elder and is consistent with similar statements found in other paragraphs of the *Discipline.*[1] It reflects the long-standing Roman Catholic/Anglican tradition out of which Methodism arose and affirms current ecumenical understandings about ordination as an elder/presbyter, but it is also distinctly United Methodist in the inclusion of "Order" and its emphasis on the covenantal nature of the elder's ministry. Paragraph 310 states, "The elders carry on the historic work of the *presbyteros* in the life of the Church. Beginning in some of the very early Christian communities, the presbyteros assisted the bishop in leading the gathered community in the celebration of sacraments and the guidance and care of its communal life. The ministry of elder exemplifies and leads the Church in service to God in the world, in remembering and celebrating the gifts of God and living faithfully in response to God's grace."

Ordained to Word and Sacrament

At least since the days of the Protestant Reformers, the tradition of the Christian church has been to ordain clergy to Word and Sacrament.[2] By ordination, persons have been entrusted with the faithful transmission of the Word and the celebration of the sacraments for the sake of the community of faith. The *Baptism, Eucharist and Ministry* document reflects the ecumenical consensus that "the chief responsibility of the ordained ministry is to assemble and build up the body of Christ by proclaiming and teaching the Word of God, by celebrating the sacraments, and by guiding the life of the community in its worship, its mission and its caring ministry."[3] In United Methodism this historic role is continued in the ministry of the ordained elder.

As we have already seen, a major motivation for John Wesley's ordinations for America was the need for sacraments among the people called Methodist since all other ministries, including preaching, could be carried out by laypersons. For both Wesley and Asbury, given their strong roots in the Anglican tradition, there was to be no administration of the sacraments without ordination. Though the Methodist movement around the world has established various ways of providing for sacramental administration by non-ordained persons under supervision of an elder in order to meet the needs of the people, until 1996 it could be said that all ordinations included some aspect of the sacramental ministry. The sacramental authority of the deacon in probation was limited, and full sacramental authority was entrusted only to the elder; but both ordinations were directly related to Word and Sacrament. In fact, prior to 1996 David Steinmetz could go so far as to say, "Ordination is for the purpose of preaching, teaching, and administrating the sacraments. Anyone who has been ordained to the ministry of the Church but who no longer is occupied with the public service of Word and sacraments is no longer performing the function for which he or she were ordained. Ordination is not a general commissioning for the service of God; that is the purpose of baptism. Ordination is so indissolubly linked to the service of Word and sacrament that it is meaningless apart from them."[4]

Steinmetz's position no longer applies to ordination in United Methodism since the new ordering of ministry broadens the meaning of ordination to include the nonsacramental ministries of the deacon. His statement, however, still applies to the ordination of elders. Regardless of the specific form or setting for ministry, the calling and the identity of the elder are always that of the sacramental representative of the Church. The elder's ministry must always embody that sacramental life, whether in a local congregation or in an extension ministry.

Both deacons and elders are ordained to Word, but this responsibility takes on specific meaning for the elder in a church with a strong emphasis on the preaching ministry. The *Book of Discipline* places specific responsibility for preaching, the Church's primary avenue for proclaiming the Word and calling the Church to its missional task, in the ministry of the elder. The elder's ministry of Sacrament is deeply rooted in the ministry of the Word. Even though the elders share with deacons the ordination to Word and share with local pastors the preaching and pastoral (including sacramental) ministry in the local congregation, the elder's calling, identity, leadership, and ministry are distinctly focused in the historic tradition of Word and Sacrament.

One of the underlying problems in discussing the ordination of the elder is the Church's failure to articulate a clear sacramental theology. It is hard to interpret the importance of ordination to Sacrament when the church has little understanding of the sacrament itself and how ordination relates to it. For Wesley, the assumption that the sacraments required ordination was foundational. But in United Methodism today, there would be limited understanding of that principle. Until we can adequately interpret a sound sacramental theology, the necessity of ordaining elders for sacramental administration will be vague and uncertain, and it will be difficult to interpret clearly the distinct role of the deacon, whose ordination does not include Sacrament.

For my purpose here I will assume the long-standing tradition of the Christian church that the sacraments should be celebrated by persons who have been called and authorized by the church through the laying on of hands by a bishop for that unique ministry. For United Methodists that is now focused in the ministry of the elder. Though the elder's ministry can be extended through the licensed local pastor in limited situations, the sacramental ministry and the primary responsibility for preaching resides in the Order of Elder.

Ordained to Order

In the creation of The United Methodist Church in 1968, Order was added to Word and Sacrament in the ordination of United Methodist deacons and elders. However, in the three decades since then, as Thomas Frank says, "much ink has been spilled about the first . . . terms, but relatively little about the last."[5] Yet whenever the ministry of the elder/presbyter is discussed in Methodism or across denominations, it includes the leadership role of administering the life of the church, the responsibility for the temporal as well as the spiritual needs of the congregation. The *Baptism, Eucharist and Ministry* document includes clear reference to the ordering aspect of the presbyter's ordination, even though it only calls for ordination to Word and Sacrament: "Presbyters serve as pastoral ministers of Word and sacraments in a local eucharistic community. They are preachers and teachers of the faith, exercise pastoral care and *bear responsibility for the discipline of the congregation to the end that the world may believe and that the entire membership of the Church may be*

102

renewed, strengthened and equipped in ministry" (italics added).[6] This would seem to be a direct reference to what United Methodists call ordination to order.

In early American Methodism the conference of traveling preachers was entrusted with the primary ordering function, but throughout the ordinal and the *Book of Discipline* across the years, it is clear that one primary task of the individual elder has been "ordering the Church for its mission and service, and administration of the *Discipline* of the Church" (¶ 303.2). In many ways the action of the 1968 General Conference makes formal a reality that was already in practice—that is, elders are set apart by ordination for the necessary leadership function of ordering the ministry and life of the Church. "Ordination," says Dennis Campbell, "is linked to the ordering and governing of the church because the care and preservation of God's faithful community has always been a sacred duty entrusted to those who will carry this out on behalf of the people in accord with the Gospel. . . . The pastor exercises the ordering task on behalf of the congregation so that it can be about its primary work of ministry in the name of Jesus Christ."[7]

Thomas Frank's description of ordination to Order and its relationship to Word and Sacrament is the best statement I have found to date, so I quote it at length:

> A ministry of Order is grounded in the Word, to be sure, as congregations and other bodies seek to bear witness to the Reign of God of which the scripture testifies. A ministry of Order is vitally linked with the sacramental life of the church as well, for the work of preparing and administering baptism and holy communion is designated to the ordained for the sake of the good order of the community. . . . But the practice of 'Order' also goes beyond Word and Sacrament. The church sets apart persons to represent the community in faith in its definite political responsibilities. They are in biblical terms stewards (*oikonomoi*) of the household (*oikos*) of faith, entrusted with making sure that every member of the house is able to serve (or minister, *diakonia*) in the most effective way possible.

Leaders ordained to Order care for the common good of the whole body. They bring to focus the concern of the whole community of faith to organize for ministry in a way that will best enable it to witness to the Reign of God. . . . Through their own gifts of leadership, they "equip . . . the saints for the work of ministry."

[T]he ministry of Order is grounded in the church's collective experience, much of which is contained in a book of canon law, order or discipline. . . . Order is inseparable from a vital and disciplined life of prayer and Christian experience.[8]

In the local congregation this ordination authorizes the elder to be the pastor in charge and lead the congregation's mission and ministry. For an elder serving as district superintendent or bishop, this ordination is lived out in the ministry of superintending the whole connection. It is one of the essential ministries of any ordained elder/presbyter and one for which United Methodist elders are distinctly set apart.

Ordained to Service

The latest addition to the ordination of the elder is the word *Service,* added by the General Conference in 1996. This decision grew out of the ongoing discussion of servant ministry and servant leadership and is a direct result of the significant changes made by the legislative committee to the ordering of ministry proposed by the bishops.

From 1784 until 1996 American Methodism followed the Anglican practice of ordaining persons first as deacons and later as elders. Thus all ordained ministers were ordained first to *diakonia* in ordination as a deacon. Full authority for the administration of the sacraments and for pastoral leadership was subsequently granted in ordination as elder. Unfortunately, this was not fully appreciated by the Church and not well understood. As we have seen, deacons were ordained as "junior elders," with little focus on the servant aspect of that ordination. The 1996 bishops' proposal attempted to define deacon's ordination as an ordi-

104

nation to service, with some deacons continuing in a lifetime of servant ministry and all elders sharing that commitment to servant leadership by first being ordained as deacons.

When the legislative committee decided to create a separate Order of Deacon in full connection and delete deacon's ordination as a prerequisite for elder's orders, there was concern about the implication for the elder's ministry. Would focusing the deacon's ministry on service in the world and the elder's ministry on sacramental administration suggest that the elder was only a sacradotal priest with little responsibility for service in the world? Restricting the ministry of elders to the internal life of the parish would be contrary to the very nature of Methodism. To address that concern, the word *Service* was added to the elders' ordination to emphasize the diaconal aspect of the elders' ministry lest they be narrowly defined as parish priests. Unfortunately, we have already heard reports of district committees and boards of ordained ministry who have mistakenly told candidates that unless they want to be a local church pastor they should become a deacon, as if the only appropriate place for an elder to serve is in the local parish and as if all specialized ministry in the world should be done by deacons.

The calling and ordination of the elder must always include a passion for the redemption of the larger community, a desire to relate the Word of God to the needs of the world, a willingness to offer oneself in service and to lead the Church in servant ministry. It is, therefore, appropriate for elders to fulfill their ordination in a variety of extension ministries as well as through pastoral ministry in the congregation. Elders in extension ministry carry the identity of the sacramental office and the apostolic proclamation of the Word into the broad reaches of society through various forms of service, but are always aware of the fullness of their ordination vows.

So the calling, identity, and leadership role of a United Methodist elder brings together these four callings: Service, Word, Sacrament, and Order, lived out in covenant community as itinerant evangelists, traveling preachers in full connection.

Ordained Itinerants Traveling the Connection

The historic terms "traveling preacher" and "traveling elder" have all but disappeared from the *Book of Discipline*. The change began in 1966 at a special conference preparing for the merger between the Evangelical United Brethren and the Methodist churches. The study committee recommended that the term "traveling preacher in full connection" be changed to "effective full-time ministerial member." Richard Heitzenrater notes that "it is interesting that what is lost in such a change are two of the key historic terms, 'traveling preacher' and 'full connection'—what is lost in that change are the basic concepts of *itineracy* and *connectionalism!*"[9]

"Traveling preacher" referred to itinerant clergy who offered themselves without reserve to travel the connection under the appointment of the bishop. The traveling preacher was always on the move, preaching, organizing, celebrating the sacraments, and overseeing the life of a large circuit, perhaps visiting particular congregations on a monthly or quarterly basis, in contrast to the local preacher who was, in fact, local. Bishop Asbury's traveling plan made a clear distinction between traveling and local preachers. Though some of his ordained elders decided to locate and withdraw from the itineracy, to be ordained included a willingness to travel the connection. With the eloquent rhetorical flourish of the 1800s, Abel Stevens describes the glorious vision of the traveling preachers:

> Away with the petty localisms of these times! Let us feel that we are one in the Lord; that our great work is not to rear up local temples, which, like the shell of the oyster, are to incrust and bind within their limits our whole ecclesiastical being, but that it is to spread holiness over the land and the world; and that every local pulsation is but the beating of the great common heart. Let the afflictions of our brethren everywhere be considered our afflictions, and their success ours.[10]

Today the practice has changed significantly and the term "traveling preacher" is seldom used, but the commitment of the ordained elder to itinerant ministry, to offer him or herself *"without reserve to be appointed and to serve"* is still very much a part of the identity and calling of the United Methodist ordained elder. Deacons in full connection may seek their own place of employment, and local pastors serve only in particular locations. Only ordained elders make the lifetime commitment to serve wherever they are appointed for the sake of the mission of the Church. Though under great strain today, Methodism's unique form of itineracy has been one of our strengths. An unmistakable mark of the identity and ministry of the elder in United Methodism is the willingness to travel the connection in lifetime service to Christ and the Church. Chapter 9 deals with itineracy in more detail.

Ordained into an Order

This itinerant ministry, however, was never intended to be lived in isolation. The single, celibate circuit rider on the frontier may have been lonely, but he was never a "lone ranger." He knew he was part of a connection, a brotherhood of persons who had committed their lives to this common ministry. Though the passion that inspired the early circuit riders may have diminished, in principle the nature of the conference membership of itinerant elders remains. Paragraph 324 expands on the covenant of elders in full connection and their commitment to itinerant ministry in one of the few places where the *Book of Discipline* rises to the level of inspiration:

> Elders in full connection with an annual conference, by virtue of their election and ordination are bound in special covenant with all the ordained elders of the annual conference. . . . They offer themselves without reserve to be appointed and to serve, after consultation, as the appointive authority may determine. They live with all other ordained ministers in mutual trust and concern and seek with them the sanctification of the fellowship.

Ordained elders relinquish membership in a local church and are not employed by the local church. Their ministry and

107

accountability is to the conference. The new ordering of ministry attempts to recover this sense of covenant in the creation of the Orders. It is yet to be seen if we can discover a new spirit-filled vitality in such a covenant community, but without this vitality the commitment the elder makes to itinerant ministry becomes a burden rather than a blessing, an obligation rather than a participation in a shared mission.

Set apart to serve as itinerant evangelists and sacramental representatives, ordering the life of the Church for its mission in the world, sent throughout the connection for the sake of the common mission, the ordained elder fulfills the ministry of Service, Word, Sacrament, and Order in order to effectively communicate the gospel and the witness or the church in the world.

CHAPTER SEVEN

Ordaining a New Deacon

*The most dramatic challenges for these churches are contin-
uing ones: to reflect on the diaconate theologically, and to
define the purpose and shape of the re-established diaconate
in light of an ancient, but broken, history and in the light of
the many needs for service in the contemporary world.*
—Rosemary S. Keller, Gerald F. Moede, and Mary E. Moore
"Called to Serve: The United Methodist Diaconate"

In recent years there has been renewed interest throughout the
Christian church in the revival of the diaconate as a service ministry in and through the church. Though the deacon is defined
quite differently in the various denominations, the focus on leadership in ministries of service is a constant factor. In some denominations the deacon is an office for lay leaders in the local church.
In others, such as those in the Anglican/Roman Catholic/
Orthodox traditions, the deacon is an ordained order that can
either be a permanent ministry or represent a time of preparation
for ordination as priest/presbyter/elder. The ordained deacon in
these traditions often serves as an assistant to or in the place of
the priest/presbyter/elder, sometimes even administering the
sacraments. The United Methodist Church has chosen to forge
something new that builds on some of these traditions and ecumenical affirmations, but is quite different from our historic office
of ordained deacon and distinct from our lay office of diaconal
minister. Dr. Kenneth Rowe of Drew Theological School says,

"The most radical change in the 1996 reordering of ministry in The United Methodist Church was the creation of a new order of deacon."[1] The deacon in full connection is in fact a new office for United Methodism and for the ecumenical church.

In *The Deacon: Ministry Through Words of Faith and Acts of Love,* Paul Van Buren and Ben L. Hartley draw on the history and the contemporary experience of newly ordained United Methodist deacons in full connection in order to assist them to interpret their ministry. The book is also an important first step in helping the Church to understand and grasp the vision of the new Order. The authors acknowledge the ambiguity of the new Order and that many new deacons are "struggling to understand their ministerial identity."[2] Clarifying and defining the ministry of the new deacon in full connection will be important not only for the deacons themselves, but for the whole Church as we move into a deeper understanding of ordination and church leadership.

The United Methodist Deacon in Full Connection: A New Creation

Robin Lovin, Dean of Perkins School of Theology, was a consultant to the Council of Bishops during the 1993–96 quadrennium and was the key writer of their report to the 1996 General Conference. He closely followed the work of the General Conference legislative committee as major changes were made in the bishops' recommendations and has continued to be involved in the implementation of our new ordering of ministry during the 1997–2000 quadrennium. In a paper addressed to the committee charged with preparing a new United Methodist ordinal, Lovin succinctly summarizes the action of the General Conference in the creation of the deacon in full connection:

In 1996, the General Conference of The United Methodist Church reordered the ministry of the denomination in light of a growing understanding that all Christians are called to ministry, and a correlative understanding that ordained ministry is primarily charged with leading others to find a place for themselves in the ministry that all Christians share. In that reordering, probably the most far-reaching change was the creation of a new order of deacon—an ordained person, a full member of the Annual Conference, non-itinerant, and called to a lifetime ministry relating the gathered life of the community to servant ministry in the world.[3]

This statement captures the overall theme of the 1996 reordering and the creation of the new office of deacon in full connection. Though this vision can be simply stated, the implementation is many-faceted and the implications are profound. Lovin goes on to say, "The starting point for my reflection . . . is that General Conference purposely created something new in the new deacon. This new order of ministry is related in name, heritage and mission to other ministries of service from the seven deacons in Acts 6 through the deacons of the early Christian communities to the deaconesses and diaconal ministers who continue to serve the church today. Yet it is also quite a new thing within the ordering of the ministry of The United Methodist Church, and it is a significant departure from the understanding of the deacon in the Roman-Anglican tradition which John Wesley adapted to the needs of the Methodist movement."[4] It is also quite different from the deacon in the Otterbein (United Brethren in Christ) tradition where the lay deacon was elected by the congregation for lay ministry to the sick and the poor.

As if to interpret by restatement, the 1996 *Book of Discipline* goes to great lengths to describe the distinct ministry of the deacon in full connection in a variety of ways, all stressing the ministry of leadership in service, rooted in the historic concept of *diakonia*:[5]

Deacons are called to ministries of Word and Service. (¶ 116)

Those who respond to God's call to lead in service and to equip others for this ministry through teaching, proclamation, and worship and who assist elders in the administration of the sacraments are ordained deacons. (¶ 303.2)

111

Within the people of God, some persons are called to the ministry of deacon. The words deacon, deaconess, and diaconate all spring from a common Greek root—*diakonos,* or "servant," and *diakonia,* or "service." Very early in its history the church, as an act of worship and praise of God, instituted an order of ordained ministers to personify or focus the servanthood to which all Christians are called. These people were named *deacons.* The ministry exemplifies and leads the Church in the servanthood every Christian is called to live both in the church and the world. The deacon embodies the interrelationship between worship in the gathered community and service to God in the world. (¶ 310)

Deacons are called by God to a lifetime of servant leadership. . . . Deacons fulfill servant ministry in the world and lead the Church in relating the gathered life of Christians to their ministries in the world, interrelating worship in the gathered community with service to God in the world. . . . It is the deacons, in both person and function, whose distinctive ministry is to embody, articulate, and lead the whole people of God in its servant ministry. (¶ 319)

Deacons are persons called by God, authorized by the Church and ordained by a bishop to a lifetime ministry of Word and Service to both the community and the congregation in a ministry that connects the two. Deacons exemplify Christian discipleship and create opportunities for others to enter into discipleship. In the world, the deacon seeks to express a ministry of compassion and justice, assisting laypersons as they claim their own ministry. In the congregation, the ministry of the deacon is to teach and to form disciples, and to lead worship together with other ordained and laypersons. (¶ 320)

This connection between service in the world and leadership in the congregation is lived out in the dual appointment of the deacon. Deacons who serve beyond the local church will also have an appointment to a local church "where they will take missional responsibility for leading other Christians into ministries of service" (¶ 322.2). If appointed within a congregation deacons must demonstrate how their ministry is leading the Church in service in the world. Wherever they are appointed, deacons must provide a written statement that clarifies their "intentionality of servant leadership in order to establish a clear distinction between the work to which all Christians are called and the work for which deacons in full connection are appropriately prepared and authorized" (¶ 322.4*b*).

I have quoted from these paragraphs at length to stress the clarity of purpose behind the creation of the office of deacon in full connection, an ordained ministry separate from that of the elder with a distinct focus on ministries of service in the world and leadership in the ministry to which all Christians are called. Unlike the former office of deacon in United Methodism, the new deacon is not ordained to the same ministry as the elder (Word, Sacrament, and Order), and is not itinerant. The office is rooted in the service ministry of the historic deacon and calls for a new understanding of this ministry.

Lovin accurately notes that the United Methodist deacon in full connection is an Order of clergy quite different from the diaconate in our Roman Catholic/Anglican heritage and the deacon of the Methodist Episcopal/Methodist/United Methodist tradition. This is true in terms of identity and ministry, but is most obvious in the deacon's relationship to the other Orders of ministry. The responsibilities of the deacon are closely related to the ministry of all Christians and carry the historic focus of the deacon on leadership in ministries of service; but the traditional understanding of the relationship between deacon, elder, and bishop is no longer appropriate for this Order.

The Deacon's Relationship to the Laity

Though ¶ 108 of the *Book of Discipline* is somewhat convoluted, it represents a legislative attempt to affirm a basic spiritual and theological conviction that underlies the ministry legislation—the unity of all ministry:

There is but one ministry in Christ, but there are diverse gifts and evidences of God's grace in the body of Christ (Ephesians 4:5-16).

113

The ministry of all Christians is complimentary. No ministry is subservient to another. All United Methodists are summoned and sent by Christ to live and work together in mutual interdependence and to be guided by the Spirit into the truth that frees and the love that reconciles.

The ways in which deacons live out their ministry in relation to the laity will be crucial in the fulfillment of this conviction since, as we have already noted, the potential for misunderstanding exists.[6] The ministry of the deacon in full connection is focused on the calling to lead the Church in ministries of service, not simply on the servant role of the individual since service in the name of Christ (*diakonia*) is the calling of all baptized Christians. Since all the functions of *diakonia* can and should be carried out by laity, ordination of the deacon is related primarily to *identity* as an ordained representative of the Church and *leadership* in the servant ministry of the entire Church,[7] otherwise we run the risk of replacing the ministry of laity with that of "ordained professionals" and contributing to the further clericalization of the Church. Ordained deacons are not intended to be super laity who take the place of or even represent the ministry of all Christians. Rather, they are called and set apart for specialized ministries of leadership within the body of Christ so that the whole ministry might be equipped for effective service in the world.

Ben Hartley and Paul Van Buren write, "A deacon's ministry must strengthen the ministry of all believers. . . . Deacons in The United Methodist Church are called, first and foremost, to lead by exemplary service and encourage lay ministry in the world and the church."[8] If we believe in the ministry of all Christians, if we believe that it is the task of every Christian to witness effectively for Christ through words of faith and acts of love, then the ordination of the deacon must undergird this ministry and not replace it.

This concern is also significant in terms of the calling and ministry of laity who serve in a variety of ministries as a vocation in the Church. The deacon is not meant to replace, for example, the deaconess. The historic ministry of laywomen called to service in the community and world on behalf of Christ and the Church is as valid today as it was in 1888 when the General Conference created the office of deaconess. Deaconesses continue to serve on the cutting edge of the Church's mission, particularly to the poor and marginalized, and their calling is not to be minimized, but rather complimented and strengthened by the ministry of ordained deacons.

Christian educators, church musicians, lay evangelists, missionaries, church business managers, child-care workers, and a host of other ministries in which laity serve in full- and part-time careers provide valid ministries that will be strengthened by the presence of deacons who understand their calling to equip these ministries in the local church and around the world.

The Deacon's Relationship to the Bishop

In terms of relationship to the bishop, the new deacon in full connection does not share the ancient deacon's identity as an assistant to or emissary of the bishop. This close bond was originally symbolized by the fact that the bishop alone would ordain a deacon, while the collegium of presbyter/priests joined the bishop in ordaining a new presbyter. This image of the deacon does not fit the new United Methodist deacon for several reasons. First, since they will be intentionally scattered in the world on behalf of the Church, deacons will not be as closely linked with the bishop as were the early deacons, who directly assisted the bishop and served at the bishop's command. Their ministry is to serve in the world representing the Church, and by design they will not be serving on a day-to-day basis in close proximity to the bishop. Their first accountability will likely be to the agency, institution, corporation, or congregation in which they are employed. Lovin says, "The fact is that most United Methodist deacons will serve in congregational or other settings in which they are primarily accountable to their employers. Because they are not itinerant, United Methodist deacons will typically have a less direct relationship to the bishop than the itinerant elders."[9]

Second, the ministry of the deacon in full connection is to be valued as a valid ministry in its own right and is not defined by a subservient relationship to the bishop. Some historians believe that the tendency for the diaconate to be seen in a subservient role as assistant to the bishop may well have contributed to its decline.[10] Whatever the history, it was certainly not in the mind of the General Conference for the diaconate to be understood as a servant to the bishop or to be defined by this relationship.

Third, since deacons are not ordained to Order, their relationship to the bishop will be different from the relationship among bishops and elders, who share a common ordination. Bishops will be elected from the ranks of the elders based on their common calling to order the Church for its mission and service, to administer the *Discipline* of the Church (¶ 303.2), and to administer the sacraments, which are of the very essence of the ministry of a bishop. Since United Methodist bishops are not ordained to a separate Order, their ordination remains that of an elder'service, Word, Sacrament, and Order. United Methodist bishops are understood to be elders who have been consecrated for leadership, undertaking the general superintendency within the whole connection (¶ 404.1). The distinct ministry of the deacon is to Word and Service and does not include Sacrament and Order, which are shared by elders and bishops. Deacons are accountable to the bishop for their ministry and for the fulfillment of their ordination vows; through their appointment by the bishop they have a direct relationship with the bishop as general superintendent.

The Deacon's Relationship to the Elder

For United Methodists who come out of Methodist Episcopal and Methodist Episcopal, South, traditions, there was a direct relationship between the deacon and the elder since candidates were ordained deacon prior to being ordained elder. John Wesley was ordained in this tradition as an Anglican priest, and from the Christmas Conference of 1784 until 1996, we continued this tradition inherited from the Church of England.

One positive aspect of this tradition was the interrelatedness of the two ordinations and their dependence on each other. The weakness was that even though some deacons served for a lifetime in that office, ordination as a deacon came to be viewed as transitional rather than as an ordination with its integrity rooted in servanthood; thus the ministry of the deacon became subsumed in the ministry of the elder. The report of the bishops to the 1996 General Conference tried to resolve this inequity by clearly defining the deacon's ordination as a ministry of service and by affirming the ministry of those who would serve as deacons for a lifetime. At the same time, the bishops recommended that elders be ordained deacon prior to elder's ordination to make clear that servanthood is basic to all ordained ministry. As we have already seen, the legislative committee revised this report by calling for a separate Order of Deacon and direct ordination of the elder. Therefore, just as the office of deacon cannot be defined by its relationship to the bishop, it also can no longer to be understood by its relationship to the elder. Though deacons share with elders the ordination to Word and Service, the Order of Deacon is meant to be distinct from the Order of Elder.

This distinction is particularly important at the point of sacramental administration since this is one of the most visible points at which the unique ministries of the deacon and the elder can be modeled and lived out. Any formulation of the deacon's ministry (for example, deacons serving as local pastors or administrating the sacraments) that makes the deacon look like a junior elder or a substitute for the elder undercuts the new Order of Deacon as a ministry of Word and Service with its own identity and integrity. At the same time such a formulation undercuts the unique ordination of elders to Sacrament and the link between ordination and sacramental administration.

The question of what role deacons play in the sacramental ministry is a matter of continued exploration and will necessarily be part of the consultations sponsored by the Division of Ordained Ministry during the 2001–2004 quadrennium. The *Book of Discipline* makes it clear that only elders are ordained for the administration of the sacraments, but it says that deacons assist in administering the sacraments (¶ 303.2). There is much discussion about the meaning of the word *assist* and the extent to which a deacon should actively participate in administering the sacraments. *Worship Matters*, a new publication on worship from the General Board of Discipleship, includes a helpful chapter entitled "The Role of Deacons and Assisting Ministers," in which authors Daniel Benedict and Anne Burnette Hook (one an elder, the other a deacon) provide a foundational principle: "The liturgical leadership role of deacons and elders serves the church best when the distinctives of each order are not glossed, but are enacted with clarity and charity."[11] Though they affirm that presiding at the table in Holy Communion is not appropriate for the deacon, the authors leave open the question of the deacon's role in baptism: "A deacon may assist an elder with the baptism ritual. Based on historical and theological grounds, it is currently unclear what the limitations on such assistance should be."[12]

The deacon's role at the table and at the font needs in-depth discussion, reviewing both the historical and the theological grounds and taking into account the ways in which we can model the distinct ministry of both the deacon and the elder. Part of the discussion involves an understanding of the sacraments and the fundamental question of what it means to be ordained to administer them. The deacon may assist in many ways, but if we are going to maintain any meaningful link between sacrament and ordination we must be clear about what one is authorized to do through ordination. Given the historic Roman Catholic/Anglican/Wesleyan/Methodist emphasis on the importance of the sacraments being celebrated by persons properly ordained to do so, a cursory understanding of their administration would seem to imply that in Holy Communion the elder is responsible for presiding at the table, the prayer of consecration, and the offering of the elements to the congregation. Distribution may be done by deacons and "assisting ministers" (laity). In baptism, administration of the sacrament would seem to mean presiding and applying the water with the words "I baptize you." I would suggest that these are symbolic acts entrusted to the elder by ordination and that assisting would then mean that deacons and laity could participate in all other aspects of the liturgy.

What is important is that in leading worship and in the celebration of the sacraments we model the shared ministry of elders, deacons, and laity together. The role each one plays should help the congregation to understand the distinct ministry of the deacon and the elder and should witness to the ministry of all Christians. Particularly in relation to the new deacon, Benedict and Hook suggest that "the role of the deacon in liturgy is to mirror his or her vocation in the world . . . to serve, to care for, to help."[13] Each has a distinct role to play for the sake of good order and the Church's ministry, but we all gather at the table to be nourished for *diakonia,* our ministry of service and witness in the world for the sake of Jesus Christ.

For United Methodists who come out of the Evangelical and United Brethren traditions, the notion of direct ordination of elders would be familiar since this was the practice of the Evangelical United Brethren Church. At this point the new legislation seems to reflect the Reformed tradition of Otterbein rather than the Anglican tradition of Wesley and Asbury. The deacon in full connection, however, would be a new concept for former Evangelical United Brethren as well as for Methodist Episcopal and Methodist Protestant streams in United Methodism.

Elders/Deacons/Bishops: Establishing a New Relationship

Having stressed the independence of the new deacon from the bishop and the elder, the urgent question then becomes "What *is* the relationship of the deacon to the bishop and the elder?" How are we to avoid a splintering of ordained ministry and a divided clergy? Let me suggest several ways in which the new Orders are related:

Commitment to a common mission

Both deacons and elders are "called by God to a lifetime of servant leadership in specialized ministries among the people of

God. . . . [and to] devote themselves wholly to the work of the Church and to the upbuilding of the ministry of all Christians" (¶ 116). Ultimately, both deacons and elders share a common hope "that all persons will be brought into a saving relationship with God through Jesus Christ and be renewed after the image of their creator" (¶ 105). A shared sense of mission unites deacon and elder in common leadership for the sake of the effective witness of Christ in the world and the fulfillment of the church's mission to make disciples of Jesus Christ.

Ordination to Word and Service

Both ordinations include the commitment to Word and Service, providing a common center for all ordained ministry. Together the ordained clergy are entrusted with the faithful transmission of the Word of God from generation to generation and both are committed to leadership in service: "Those who respond to God's call to *lead in service* and to equip others for this ministry through teaching, proclamation, and worship and who assist the elders in the administration of the sacraments are ordained deacons. Those whose *leadership in service* includes preaching and teaching the Word of God, administration of the sacraments, ordering the Church for its mission and service, and administration of the *Discipline* of the Church are ordained as elders" (¶ 303.2; italics added). Both are called to devote themselves to "a lifetime of servant leadership in specialized ministries among the people of God" (¶ 116).

Because deacons and elders are rooted in this common ministry, Ben Hartley suggests that the distinction between the two is a matter of focus: "Deacons are more focused on inter-relating the altar and the marketplace and the *diakonia* function of the church, whereas elders are more focused on the *kerygma* and the apostolic function of the church."[14] The deacon focuses on Service and the elder focuses on Word, but both share these common elements of their ordination.

120

Membership in the clergy session

Chapter 9 will discuss conference membership, but at this point it is sufficient to say that in the development of Methodism in America, conference membership has usually taken precedence over ordination as the defining reality. Clergy are not ordained outside the covenant of conference membership, but must first be received as members of the annual conference. Ordination takes place within the context of the covenant community of the annual conference (¶ 324). The fact that both deacons and elders will be accountable to one clergy session and will be acting on all matters related to ordained ministry in one body is a significant symbol of the unity of ministry. Though the two Orders are distinct, they are not separate, but share this common covenant community as their primary place of membership and accountability within the body of Christ.

Also, candidates for ordination as elder and deacon share in a common candidacy, basic elements of theological education, and probationary period when they are, in effect, neither deacons nor elders, but all are "commissioned ministers." These commonalities can strengthen the ties between them as new classes of ordinands experience this process.

Accountability to the bishop

Though the way in which their accountability is lived out differs, the fact remains that both deacons and elders will be accountable to the same general superintendency, the bishop and the district superintendent. Elders continue to be itinerant and therefore dependent on and accountable to the bishop for their place of service (¶ 329).

Except for elders serving in extension ministries who may be hired by a local agency, elders are not hired by the local church to which they are appointed. Deacons are able to initiate their own employment and will be hired by the local church or agency in which they serve. As members in full connection, however, deacons are also appointed by the bishop, and the bishop has clear authority over that appointment. "If the bishop and cabinet consider an appointment not to be in the best interest of the Church, the bishop may choose not to make the appointment. In such event, the bishop shall be in consultation with the deacon and the board of ordained ministry. The deacon in full connection shall then seek another appointment, request a leave of absence, relinquish his or her credentials, or be terminated by disciplinary procedures" (¶ 322.4c).

One of the distinct differences between the ordained deacon and the diaconal minister, deaconess, or layperson serving in specialized ministry careers in the Church comes precisely at this point of accountability. For the diaconal minister, the place of service was to be approved by the bishop. For the deacon in full connection, the bishop's appointment is, in fact, an appointment and is fulfilled at the bishop's discretion for the sake of the total ministry of the Church. Though they are not itinerant and can initiate their places of service, deacons are sent by the bishop and serve under the authority of the episcopal office. The way in which appointments of deacons and elders are made may vary, but both are accountable to the bishop for their ministry and service. Please see appendix 5 for detailed information on the appointment of the deacon in full connection from the Section of Deacons and Diaconal Ministers in the Division of Ordained Ministry.

The new ordering of ministry affirms the unique ministries of laity, deacons, elders, and bishops, and it demands a partnership in ministry that must be modeled by the ordained leaders of the church. Building these new relationships will be the challenge and the opportunity of the next generation as we live into these new forms of ministry.

CHAPTER EIGHT

The Evolution of the Local Preacher to Local Pastor

It cannot be doubted that in almost every instance, they have gone before the regular ministry, carrying the Gospel, where the others were not able, or prepared to carry it; taking up appointments in the sparsely settled part of the country and maintaining them until they could be taken into the regular work of the traveling preachers.

—Anonymous address to Local Preachers Association, 1866
Frederick Norwood, *Ministry in the Methodist Heritage*

Wesley's and Asbury's Lay Preachers

From the early days of Wesley's revival to the present, the ministry of the lay preacher has been crucial to the Methodist movement's evangelistic mission and to the pastoral care of the people called Methodist in England, America, and around the world. But the place of the local preacher in the ordering of ministry has been a matter of great debate, and the evolution of the local preacher to the current local pastor in United Methodism has been a significant transition. To understand the origins of this ministry in Methodism, it is necessary to establish two important distinctions: first, the distinction between the sacramental ministry and the preaching ministry; and second, the distinction between the traveling ministry and the local ministry. Frederick Norwood confirms that "Methodism has always possessed not one ministry, but two. They may be described as ordained and lay, or in a more specially American context, as traveling and local."[1]

For Wesley, as we have already seen, there was a clear distinction between the preaching and the sacramental, the prophetic and the priestly, the lay and the ordained ministry. He called forth and organized a cadre of lay preachers and class leaders to carry on the revival, organize class meetings, serve the needy in the world, and care for the pastoral needs of the Methodists within the societies, but the sacramental ordinances were carried out by ordained Anglican priests. In America early Methodist lay leaders and preachers like Captain Webb and Barbara Heck organized and led societies; but, as in England, Methodists were expected to rely on episcopally ordained clergy for the sacraments, and the distinction between the preaching ministry and the ordained, sacramental ministry was continued.

Asbury drew a sharp distinction between the traveling ministry and the local ministry, with the willingness to itinerate being the defining mark. One ministry was "derived from the Great Commission," says Norwood, "and the other from the priesthood of all believers."[2] Local preachers were laity and were *local*. They were assigned to preach where they lived, either working as an advance team for the traveling preacher or carrying on the ministry between visits of the traveling elder, who would provide the sacramental ministry and oversee the life of the circuit. The local preacher was authorized to preach in that congregation, but was not a member of the conference or entitled to a regular appointment and in most cases did not provide sacramental ministry. The position was often a first step toward the traveling ministry. Norwood says "The steps then would follow: member, class leader, exhorter, local preacher, traveling preacher on trial, traveling deacon, and finally, traveling elder."[3]

To understand the importance of the local preacher in early Methodism, one need only consider the numbers. Norwood reports that in 1784, at the time of the Christmas Conference, there were eighty-three itinerants and several hundred local preachers. In 1812 there were about 700 traveling and 2,000 local preachers, and by 1840 there were 3,413 itinerants compared to 6,339 locals. In 1854 the number of local preachers had increased to 8,500. He concludes:

> It would be hard to exaggerate the importance of the work of the local preachers in the period before the Civil War. Time and again, we learn that the circuit rider, bravely leading the way into unchart-ed wilderness to carve out a new circuit, arrived to discover that a local preacher had already been there and organized a class. In fact, likely as not, the itinerant found much-needed food, lodging, and companionship in the cabin of a local preacher.[4]

Some lay preachers were untrained and inexperienced, with lit-tle more than a heart warmed by grace and a call to preach. Some were well-educated professional persons who could not itinerate on a full-time basis, e.g., Edward Tiffin, first governor of Ohio, who was ordained a local deacon by Asbury and retained his license to preach throughout his career in public office. Some were traveling preachers who located, giving up itinerancy and their membership in the annual conference, yet retaining their orders, often because of the decision to marry.

It is important to note that early in Methodism provisions were made for local pastors to seek ordination and thereby be author-ized to celebrate the sacraments. As early as 1798 local pastors could be ordained as local deacons. The *Book of Discipline* of that year states: "A local preacher shall be eligible for the office of deacon, after he has preached for four years from the time he received a regular license."[5] And in 1812 local deacons were allowed to become local elders after four years of service as a local deacon. They had sacramental authority by right of their ordination, but they did not itinerate and therefore were not members of the conference. This provision kept faith with the Wesleyan conviction that there should be no sacramental admin-istration without ordination and met the pragmatic need for sacraments in congregations served by local preachers. It created the strange figure, however, of an ordained layperson, a contra-diction in terms for a church whose ordination was rooted in the

Roman Catholic/Anglican tradition. Bishop Ann Sherer and Robert Kohler conclude: "We lived with this oxymoron of an ordained lay local preacher for nearly one hundred eighty years, and it was not until 1976 that the General Conference . . . abolished the office."[6] By and large, however, the dual ministry of ordained traveling elders and unordained local preachers effectively served the needs of this growing evangelistic movement that was able to expand and move with the frontier.

Local Preachers in the Second Century

This dual ministry worked well for Methodism's first century. The crisis came when the circuit rider dismounted and located into a given community. With the settling of the traveling elder in one place, the local preacher, local deacon, local elder, and to some degree the class leaders and exhorters were displaced. The locals were "considered to be second-string preachers whose usefulness was sadly limited," says Frederick Norwood.[7] This change resulted in confusion concerning the identity of the elder as well as undermining the role of the local preachers. Formerly, the distinguishing mark of the traveling elder was itineracy, conference membership, and full sacramental authority. When elders settled they were often working side by side with local preachers; and because the sacraments were not central to Methodist worship, the only distinction the laity could see was conference membership. The earlier distinctions between preaching and sacramental, lay and ordained, traveling and local ministries were blurred as some congregations were served by ordained elders, some by unordained local preachers, and some by ordained lay preachers!

The pressure mounted for the unordained local preacher as well as the ordained local deacon and local elder to be able to serve the sacraments in their congregation. Finally, in 1926 the Methodist Episcopal Church, South, for the first time in American Methodism, granted unordained local preachers authority "in the absence of an elder or Bishop, to administer baptism and the sacrament of the Lord's Supper with the understanding that no permanent powers of ordination are conferred until granted by the laying on of hands."[8] The Methodist Episcopal Church did not permit unordained local preachers to celebrate the Lord's Supper, but it did permit them to baptize. The practice continued unchanged in the Methodist Episcopal Church, South, until 1939; and in the merger with the Methodist Episcopal and Methodist Protestant churches, the newly formed Methodist Church allowed that "unordained Local Preachers, only while serving as regularly appointed Pastors of Charges, shall be authorized to administer the Sacraments of Baptism and of the Lord's Supper."[9]

In 1964 the Study Committee on the Ministry offered a proposal to prohibit unordained persons from administering the sacraments, but it was defeated by the General Conference. Four years later in the 1968 merger with the Evangelical United Brethren, the title was changed from local preacher to lay pastor, emphasizing their lay status. The prohibition on sacramental administration was included, only to be reversed again in 1976 due to the practical problems that resulted in the many charges served by what in that year became known as local pastors. That conference also discontinued ordination as local deacon. This is clearly one of the places where the various strands of our history and tradition—South and North, Reformed and Anglican, lay and ordained—came into conflict and blended in a fascinating and strange way. Methodism's pragmatic response to the needs of the church moved in harmony and in contradiction, with the hope that the result would be effective ministry.

Local Pastors Today

In 1980 local pastors under full-time appointment were granted clergy membership in the annual conference, and in 1996 the definition of clergy was adapted to include part-time as well as full-time local pastors: *"Clergy* in the United Methodist Church are individuals who serve as commissioned ministers, deacons, elders, and local pastors under appointment of a bishop (full- and part-time), who hold membership in an annual conference, and who are commissioned, ordained, or licensed" (¶ 119). The local preacher's transition from lay to clergy was complete. Local preachers are now clergy, even though they are not ordained, and are members of the annual conference, even though they do not itinerate. The two early distinctions between the sacramental and the preaching ministries and the traveling and the local ministries have been radically altered.

Another significant change in 1996, as we have already seen, is that the local pastor license will be used to credential all commissioned ministers serving as pastors during their three years of probation. Though this is similar to the practice of the former Evangelical United Brethren Church, it means that what was considered a missional exception (unordained ministers with sacramental authority) has become the norm for all those seeking elder's ordination.

Also, since the category of deacon has been redefined as a separate Order of Word and Service, it is no longer appropriate for local pastors to be ordained deacon and received as associate members.[10] Therefore, a way has been provided for local pastors to move toward ordination as elder and full membership in the annual conference. This change affirms the importance of the local pastor, but it was not intended to become a replacement or an alternative for the seminary route to ordination. It is yet to be seen what the results will be, but it is obvious that United Methodism is in a time of radical change in regard to the ministry of unordained local pastors and their relationship to ordained elders. The 1996 General Conference did not settle the question, but, rather, reopened the unresolved issues of ordination, sacraments, and the appropriate use of unordained clergy.

Conclusion

This brief account of the evolution of the local preacher/lay pastor/local pastor from a lay ministry to clergy indicates something of the ambiguity of the Church on these matters. Particularly in regard to the sacramental ministry of the local pastor, Dennis Campbell concludes:

> The confusing provisions made by Methodism to allow unordained pastors to administer the sacraments is at once inconsistent with Wesley and consistent with American Methodism's appropriation of the Wesley tradition. The inconsistency is clear. Wesley's extraordinary ordinations were done precisely to avoid administration without ordination. The consistency is that American Methodism emphasized the Wesleyan concern for flexibility in the face of practical need.[11]

Without a doubt the ministry of the local pastor will continue to be vital and an important way to provide pastoral leadership to small membership churches in rural and inner-city settings and for missional ethnic minority congregations. In 1997 there were 1,700 full-time and 2,800 part-time local pastors serving the connection. Though the number of local pastors fluctuates based on the number of elders and the need of local churches, the role of the local pastor will continue to be a valued ministry in United Methodism for the future. We are no longer on the frontier, and traveling elders are fully settled in local appointments alongside local pastors. It is no longer a lay ministry, but a clergy ministry. What impact this will have on the ministry of the elder, the meaning of conference membership, and itineracy is still uncertain. It is certain that Methodism will continue to seek pragmatic, effective ways of providing ministry in the face of practical need and for the sake of the local congregations. This is the missional ministry of the local pastor.

CHAPTER NINE

Conference Membership, Itineracy, and Ordination

Itineracy of Methodist preachers, beginning with John Wesley himself, was the result of Wesley's principle that he should preach wherever he could do the most good. Or to state it another way, he should preach wherever there was a need and especially where the need was greatest.
—Richard P. Heitzenrater in *Connectionalism: Ecclesiology, Mission and Identity, United Methodism in American Culture*

In his text on United Methodist polity, Thomas Frank acknowledges that "no aspect of United Methodist polity and practice is richer in history and lore, denser with traditions and expectations, or more difficult to interpret than the ministries of pastoral and diaconal leadership in the church." He puts the changes of the 1996 ministry legislation in perspective by reminding us that "when the 1996 General Conference adopted a plan of ministry radically departing from over two hundred years of Methodist tradition, it introduced only the latest in a long line of controversies that result from an ever-shifting synthesis of understandings."[1] Some of the most significant changes resulting from this legislation have to do with the relationship between conference membership, itineracy, and ordination, basic elements in Methodism's ministry and central to our denominational identity and self-understanding.

The Dual Framework: Conference Membership and Ordination

Frank introduces a helpful term in describing the relationship of conference membership to ordination: the "dual or double framework."[2] He reminds us that Wesley and the early Methodist movement emphasized the preaching ministry of itinerant lay preachers and moved to forms of ordination primarily because of the pressing need for sacraments:

> As a consequence of privileging preaching and the pragmatic roots of ordination, United Methodism continues to authorize the ministry of pastors in two separate, sometimes parallel, sometimes discordant frameworks. The one with clear priority, as demonstrated often by the grammar of the *Discipline*, is annual conference relationship. The other is ordination, which derives its importance not so much from its intrinsic value as from its relationship with credentials for full conference membership.[3]

In early Methodism, admission to conference membership and ordination were essentially unrelated. Wesley's first conference was made up entirely of lay preachers, and the conferencing of Methodist lay preachers in America predated the ordinations at the 1784 Christmas Conference. What defined Methodist preachers was conference membership based on the willingness to preach and travel in the itinerate evangelistic ministry. If they located, they relinquished their membership in the conference.

Gradually, however, ordination became "the distinguishing mark of full conference members,"[4] and the meaning of "traveling" changed, as well. As the traveling preachers settled into communities, the term no longer meant constantly riding the circuit, but rather to be "traveling preachers in full connection" symbolized a covenant based on a willingness to be appointed and sent wherever needed. To travel was to be available, to "offer them-

131

selves without reserve, to be appointed and to serve" (¶ 324). Through many changes across the years, this basic commitment to be sent, rather than to be called or to initiate their own appointment, characterized the covenant of Methodist clergy. Though distinct in themselves, conference membership (including the commitment to itineracy) and ordination became inextricably related, though conference membership continued to be the defining reality.

This dual framework, at least in principle, was grounded in shared values that gave meaning to the rigors and demands of itineracy. These values include a sense of shared mission, a priority on the connection rather than on the local, and mutual accountability to each other in the covenant community.

A Strategy for Shared Mission

An understanding of itineracy begins with the missional mandate that gave rise to this distinctly Methodist way of ordering ministry. Russell Richey suggests:

> Connectionalism actualizes a missional principle, a principle expressed perhaps best by itineracy and general superintendency. Itineracy has meant that the connection has first claim on the itinerants and the connection makes its claim on behalf of its purpose, namely, "to reform the Continent, and spread scriptural Holiness over these Lands." Connectionalism and itineracy constitute the church as missionary by nature.[5]

Itineracy was first and foremost an evangelistic mission strategy, with clergy being sent, rather than called, "out of a passionate desire to share the gospel, to save souls, to go where the people are—*all people*, not just one class or segment of society."[6] It meant breaking down the parochial, narrow boundaries of culture or geography. On the American frontier this passionate commitment to a common mission compelled a monasticlike order of young, male, circuit-riding preachers to take up a sacrificial, celibate lifestyle and to give themselves "without reserve" to the work. To be a conference member was to be itinerant. To be itinerant was to share in the missional strategy for proclaiming the gospel. Within the context of itinerant conference membership, ordination authorized persons for specific ministry including the sacraments. None of it would have made sense without the common mission that undergirded the system.

It is interesting to note that the first *Book of Discipline* for the Methodist Church following the merger of 1939 included this question for preachers on trial: "Will you keep before you as the one great objective of your life the advancement of God's Kingdom?"[7] The candidate's commitment to the shared mission was central to conference membership and ordination. Unfortunately, that question is no longer asked in as direct a form. Clergy candidates are asked if they have examined our polity and discipline and agree with them, and a shared vision is evident in the paragraphs describing the mission of the Church, but clergy are not asked about their commitment to a specific mission or to a motivating vision shared by all in full connection.

Rather, more recent editions of the *Book of Discipline* tend to focus on the responsibilities of ordained clergy *within* the Church, as those who interpret the needs of the world, equip the Church for ministry, embody servanthood, fulfill the priestly function, and provide oversight for the Church's mission. But the missional mandate propelling clergy into witness in the world has been diminished. Though unintended, the emphasis on servant leadership could contribute to an overemphasis on a somewhat passive role of clergy inside the Church, rather than as itinerant evangelists on the vanguard of missional outreach in the world. The historic commitment to a shared mission reflecting the passionate desire to "reform the Continent, and spread scriptural Holiness over these Lands" appears to be missing as a central element of conference membership and ordination. Without this commitment, offering oneself "without reserve" to an itinerant ministry loses its power.

Instead of being understood as a missional strategy, itineracy is all too frequently seen as a maintenance system by both clergy and congregations. For clergy, conference membership is equated with job security, rather than being understood as a self-giving, sacrificial response to a missional calling. For congregations, the assurance of pastoral leadership that itineracy provides is seen as congregational maintenance, rather than as an identification with the broader mission of the whole connection. Bishop William Oden concludes, "In less than two centuries we have moved from the Asburyan frontier itineracy . . . to a settled itineracy . . . we have had a radical shift from the priority of saving souls . . . and serving the poor to a priority of pastoral care within the flock."[8] The loss of a common evangelistic missional mandate undercuts itineracy, robs conference membership of its vitality, and creates maintenance ministry in local churches.

Donald Treese, former Associate General Secretary of the Division of Ordained Ministry, quotes a district superintendent who said, "The lack of a clear articulated missional basis for itineracy is eroding it from within as nothing else!"[9] If the dual framework is to be renewed, it will begin with a clear sense of mission shared by those who are sent in itinerant ministry and the local congregations they serve for the sake of the mission of the whole connection.

The creation of the new office of deacon in full connection is intended to focus on the Church's ministry in service and to expand the ways in which we deploy persons for the mission of the Church. The whole ordering of ministry, as we have seen, assumes that service is the defining mark of ministry; and the deacon is called to embody that commitment. Even though they do not share in the covenant of itineracy, if deacons can, by their life and work, draw the Church's attention to the missional needs of the world, if they can "personify or focus the servanthood to which all Christians are called," and if their ministry "exemplifies and leads the Church in the servanthood every Christian is called to live both in the church and the world" (¶ 310), then they could help to call the Church once again to this common mission. If deacons, however, join many elders in seeing conference membership as a support system for clergy, rather than as a sending system for the mission of Christ, we will only compound our malaise.

Let me quickly say that I believe that there is a need for support systems for clergy. That is the motivation for the call for an Order of Elders and an Order of Deacons in each annual conference. But if conference membership is seen primarily as a tenure track with guarantee of salary and benefits; if the Orders become lobbying groups for their members; if itineracy and episcopal appointment are viewed as job security rather than as a missional strategy, we will never see the revival of Methodism as a movement capable of bringing new life and holiness to the world. For deacons and elders alike, a sense of our shared mission must undergird the understanding of conference membership; and specifically for elders, a new commitment to itineracy will come only with a renewed sense of our call to *go!* Go into all the world, go wherever needed, go to travel the connection in order to proclaim the gospel and make disciples for Jesus Christ. For Wesley and Asbury, Otterbein and Albright, the evangelistic task of spreading the revival was the first priority. The renewal of itineracy and conference membership will not come without the same sense of a shared mission in the name and spirit of Jesus Christ.

The Priority of the Connection

When commissioned ministers are received as probationary members of an annual conference, they are no longer laity, no longer members of a local church; rather, their very identity as a member of Christ's church is related to their membership in the covenant community of clergy. When they are ordained and become members in full connection they relinquish the local for the sake of the connection. Indeed, even though the annual conference now includes lay members, it is not primarily "a covenant body of congregations, but as an order of preachers accountable to each other for their conduct and effectiveness. Lay persons have been full participants in conference only since the 1930s, and the Constitution first required equal numbers of lay and clergy members in annual conference only in 1976."[10]

This is not to minimize the importance of laity in the annual conference, but it is to say that for clergy annual conference membership should mean something entirely different than it does for the lay members who are first members of the local church, then elected by that local church as members of the annual conference. Laity participation in the annual conference does not effect their basic membership in the Church, which is through their local congregation and hence the connection of United Methodism. For clergy, membership in the conference takes precedence over identification with any specific local church. The annual conference clergy session becomes, in a very real way, their congregation.

Clergy are then sent on behalf of the connection, for the sake of the mission, to particular places of service, with the place and duration of their appointment determined by the bishop with concern for the whole connection. Russell Richey says, "Ministers are sent, and they are sent where most needed. . . . So ministers are ordained in the conference because the call is not to some locale but to mission, to the connection, to the world." Referring to the history of the Church he adds, "Methodism, with its principles of itineracy and connectionalism, elaborated a national, frontier-oriented, ministry-delivery-system. With its orientation to the whole, to continent and world, Methodism early adopted new mechanisms that took or brought the Gospel to those who needed it."[11] Thus to be a clergy member in full connection means that the connection takes precedence; and ministry in a particular locale is to be seen as a part of the larger mission, rather than the center of mission. For elders, this is dramatically acted out in the covenant of itinerancy.

In the context of our historic identity and contemporary ferment, Thomas Frank says:

> The 1996 General Conference adopted new forms of ministry that will shake the dual framework to its foundations. For the first time in Methodist history, there is an ordained order of persons who do not itinerate and who initiate their own place of employment. Deacons are ordained to "Word and Service," including "proclamation of the Word" (¶¶ 319, 320). But this preaching and service ministry does not participate in the historic understanding of the missionary order of Methodist preachers willing to go where sent.

(Local pastors do not have to itinerate either, but they do not initiate their employment).[12]

The *Book of Discipline* makes clear that the appointment of the deacon "may be initiated by the individual deacon in full connection, the agency seeking their service, the bishop, or the district superintendent" (¶ 322.4*a*). Having found a place of service, the deacon will then seek appointment by the bishop to that setting. The bishop may choose not to make the appointment, but the deacon's employment in that place is not necessarily dependent on the bishop's approval. Elders will continue to be fully itinerant, "the accepted method of The United Methodist Church by which ordained elders are appointed by the bishop to fields of labor" (¶ 329). The other side of the deacons' freedom to initiate their place of service is the fact that the deacon, though a member in full connection, has no assurance of a place of service within the connection. The polity that provides creative freedom for deacons also leaves them somewhat vulnerable, with no guarantee of a place to serve.

Since the vision for the new deacon in full connection is of persons serving in far-flung ministries in the world, rather than primarily within the congregation, this style of deployment seems appropriate, enabling persons to serve as ordained representatives of the Church in diverse settings far beyond the places where the Church has authority. It provides flexibility for the deacon and frees the conference from the obligation of appointment. My point here is simply that full conference membership that does not include the covenant of itineracy and the assurance of an appointment within the connection represents a radical change in Methodist polity and calls for a new understanding of the priority of the connection.

As already noted, for clergy members in full connection, conference membership takes the place of local church membership, and their commitment to the ministry of the connection takes precedence over ministry in a specific congregation. Under the new legislation both deacons and elders give up local church membership and place their membership in the annual conference.

For the elder, the call continues to be, as Russell Richey says, "not to some locale but to mission, to the connection, to the world."[13] Though it is possible for the deacon, on the other hand, to be hired by a local congregation or agency, then appointed by the bishop, the commitment to the connection needs to be just as clear.

Today an emphasis on localism and a creeping congregationalism threatens to undercut this historic commitment to the larger mission and the priority of the connection. In reviewing the 1996 *Book of Discipline*, Thomas Frank notes that "the local church has been moving to the forefront of the *Discipline* through much of the last century. It now comes first in the 'Organization and Administration' division (Part V) . . . United Methodism would seem to be focused increasingly on the ministry and mission of the local church, and on the local church as the primary expression of the whole church's mission."[14] Today the local church's relationship to the connection is a point of creative energy and conflicted tension. In such a time it is critical that all ordained clergy, both itinerant elders and non-itinerant deacons, have a broad vision of the ministry of the Church and what it means to be in full connection. This issue has significant implications for the future of itineracy and our understanding of the dual framework.

A Covenant of Mutual Accountability

Full conference membership assumes a covenant of mutual accountability. All clergy are accountable, not only to the bishop and the superintendents, but also to the covenant community of the clergy in full connection, the annual conference. As we have seen, this balance between the authority of the conference and the role of the episcopacy has been an important issue since the early days of the Methodist movement. Francis Asbury's decision to ask for election by the Christmas Conference prior to his ordination was a pivotal moment, striking a balance between the authoritarian leadership of John Wesley and the full dominance of the conference, as represented by the Fluvanna Conference. Clergy in full connection accept responsibility for the ordering of their life together and for the maintenance of the "highest ideals of the Christian life" (¶ 304.2) among their colleagues. "By entering into this covenant, they accept and subject themselves to the process of clergy discipline. . . . Only those shall be elected to full membership who are of unquestionable moral character and genuine piety, sound in fundamental doctrines of Christianity, and faithful in the discharge of their duties" (¶ 324).

The annual conference's task to "make inquiry into the moral and official conduct of its ordained ministers and local pastors" (¶ 605.6) becomes the agenda of the clergy session, but is usually focused in one all too perfunctory question: "Are all clergy blameless in their life and administration?" The sense of mutual accountability reflected in this question is crucial to effective connectional ministry.

Acknowledging the challenges to itineracy, the bishops' address to the 1988 General Conference lifted up the need to "redeem and renew the itineracy."[15] Donald Treese reminds us that this, of course, was not the first time such a call was given. The 1844 episcopal address sounded concern for the health of itineracy over the issue of marriage among itinerants. Even John Wesley lamented over some of his helpers who resisted itineracy. In a chapter from one of the few books dealing with itineracy, Donald Treese says, "If itineracy is to be redeemed and renewed, it cannot be done apart from the clergy covenant of the annual conference."[16] The sense of covenant among clergy is vital to a healthy itinerant system.

In characterizing this covenant, Treese says:

> The commitment called for in this covenant is a radical one. Giving up control of one's vocational life is an expression of radical obedience to God and the church. To be chosen and to agree to a servant mode of ministry—to be "under orders"—is a rare counterculture act in the final decade of the twentieth century. . . . But it need not be lived out in isolation; it should be lived out in a caring, supportive covenant relationship sometimes referred to as "the congregation of the clergy."[17]

Unfortunately, the reality is often quite different from the ideal. Many clergy do not experience conference membership as a caring, supportive covenant relationship. This reality in part motivated the bishops to recommend the creation of Orders for ordained deacons and elders. This new emphasis reclaims the original purpose of the conference as the gathering of traveling preachers for "polity, fraternity, and revival."[18] The vision is of a "covenant community within the church to mutually support, care for, and hold accountable its members for the sake of the life and mission of the church. These orders, separately or together, seek to respond to the spiritual hunger among clergy for a fulfilling sense of vocation, for support among peers during this stressful time of change in the Church, and for a deepening relationship with God" (¶ 311).

During the 1997–2000 quadrennium there have been attempts to organize the Orders in most annual conferences, but it is too early to evaluate the progress that has been made. It may take a generation for clergy to rediscover the vitality of a common mission and shared covenant among clergy in full connection; but if mutual accountability is to be anything more than a legalistic application of prescribed policies, this kind of caring covenant community will be required as its foundation.

The Division of Ordained Ministry has provided some guidelines during the 1997–2000 quadrennium to help interpret the various aspects of the deacon's and the elder's accountability. For elders appointed to local churches, accountability to the district superintendent, the bishop, and the clergy session precludes accountability to the local church. Elders in extension ministries are employed by the agency to which they are appointed, but are still itinerant and accountable to the bishop.

Because deacons are employed by a local church or agency and subsequently appointed by the bishop, their first point of accountability will likely be to the employing body. In a local church where an elder and a deacon serve together, the deacon will be employed by the congregation with accountability to the staff-parish relations committee and the pastor. The elder will be appointed by the bishop, not hired by the local church, and will supervise the deacon on staff. In terms of accountability for ministry, this makes a significant difference; but both deacons and elders are to be accountable to the general superintendency, the bishop and district superintendent, and to the clergy session.

We can hope that the presence of deacons in full connection in the clergy covenant community will call all clergy to a new commitment to service and to see themselves as missionary evangelists sent into the world, leading the whole Church in ministry for the sake of Jesus Christ. For elders, conference membership and itinerary need to be seen as a mission strategy, rather than as a support system for the members of the Order. The new ordering of ministry calls for rethinking the meaning of conference membership, the elder's commitment to itineracy, and the deacon's ordination to service in the world. We can also hope that deacons and elders will discover new forms of covenant community in the Orders, that together they will create a new clergy session that will share a common mission encompassing the needs of the whole connection, and that they will support each other in a covenant of mutual accountability.

Summary

Evaluating the New Ordering of Ministry

The mission of the Church is to make disciples of Jesus Christ by proclaiming the good news of God's grace and thus seeking the ful- fillment of God's reign and realm in the world. . . . Whenever United Methodism has had a clear sense of mission, God has used our Church to save persons, heal relationships, transform social structures, and spread scriptural holiness, thereby changing the world.

—The Book of Discipline, ¶ 200

At this early stage in the life of the new ordering of United Methodist ministry, what can be said by way of evaluation?

Fidelity to Our Tradition(s)

Richard Heitzenrater's comprehensive study of the various min- istry studies prior to 1988[1] and a review of the changes in the years leading up to 1996 demonstrate the fact that at many points we have not maintained a consistent theology or practice in regard to ordination, but, rather, that the decisions of various gen- eral conferences have responded to the needs of the times, to political pressure, and to pragmatism. At this point the action of the 1996 General Conference has some consistency with our his- tory—it demonstrates a willingness to modify and reshape our life together based on pragmatism, perceived mission, and the demands of the time. As we said at the beginning, we have often worked out practice first, then thought through the theological implications. In our better moments, or by the grace of God, this has served us well. Whether or not the changes of 1996 demonstrate the grace of God, the new ordering of ministry does represent our pragmatic approach to ministry and the creativity and confusion that sometimes result.

Having said that, it is clear we have maintained fidelity to some of the basic, essential elements of ordination. With John Wesley we continue to affirm the urgency of the inward call, the centrality of the sacraments, the need for episcopal ordination, and the conviction that all ministry must serve the missional mandate of the gospel. We part company with Wesley at the point of the Anglican tradition's between the deacon and the elder, the conviction that sacramental administration is the primary reason for ordination, and the belief that there can be no sacramental administration without ordination.

With Francis Asbury we continue to affirm the importance of ordination's being authorized by the conference and conferred through already existing ministries as represented by the bishop. The validity of ministry is confirmed by its effectiveness in fulfilling the mission of Christ, and the bishop continues to be of the same order as the elder, but differing in function. We part company with Asbury in the assumption that bishops, elders, and deacons all share in the ministry of Sacrament and in the expectation that conference membership should be based on the willingness to itinerate.

The most conspicuous break from the Roman Catholic/Anglican tradition is at the point where elders/presbyters/priests are no longer ordained deacon prior to ordination as elder. It is a significant change when one considers our history, but we have yet to see what effect it might have on our self-understanding as clergy and as a church. The fact is that prior to 1996 ordination as a deacon lacked meaning for many persons as an ordination to service. All too often it was seen as "junior elder" status; or even worse, ordination as a deacon was viewed as most important, with elder's ordination being little more than a confirmation of the early act.

In one sense our new ordering of ministry is closer to the Reformed strand of our history, represented by Philip William Otterbein—that is, we now have a single order of ordained elder. Where Otterbein saw the deacon as a lay office in the local church, however, we have created an additional Order of clergy in the form of the deacon in full connection. At most other points, there is little similarity to the Otterbein tradition, which focused on the authority of the local church rather than that of the conference.

The issues of lay empowerment that were the driving force behind the O'Kelly revolt, the Methodist Protestant Church, and other schisms, continue to be with us today, as reflected in the ongoing debate about lay participation in the laying on of hands in ordination and in the constitutional change that allows laity on the Board of Ordained Ministry to vote on clergy orders. For the first time in our history, matters of clergy orders and discipline are not restricted to those within the covenant, but now include the voice and vote of laity. This may well be one of the healthiest changes made by the 1996 Conference in breaking down the sense of separation and elitism that has surrounded the clergy session. However, when persons who do not share in the vows of ordination, who are not under orders or itinerant, and who do not share the same accountability to the *Discipline* are involved in the ordering function, the principle that the ordained will "maintain the ministerial standards established by those in the covenant" (¶ 324) could be compromised. The annual conference clergy session is no longer the exclusive community of traveling preachers in full connection, so the creation of the new Orders should meet that need.

In creating the new office of deacon in full connection we are, in the words of Robin Lovin, "doing a new thing." This Order maintains continuity with the essential service ministry of the deacon and is consistent with other branches of Christianity where deacons are ordained to a lifetime of servant ministry, devoting themselves "wholly to the work of the Church and to the upbuilding of the ministry of all Christians" (¶ 116). The creation of an ordained clergy office that is non-sacramental, however, moves away from the ecumenical consensus. For Methodists, full clergy membership in the annual conference apart from itineracy is a significant change; and the appointment of one who is not directly employed by the Church in far-flung places of service where the bishop has little authority and the person is accountable to another agency is a new venture. Though the new Order of Deacon builds on the long history of the deaconess and the relatively brief history of the lay worker and the diaconal minister, the fact that the office is an ordained ministry makes it unlike these lay offices. Though clearly linked with important elements of our tradition, the deacon in full connection is distinct to United Methodism, calling for a new definition of ordination.

The Order of Elder continues the historic link between ordination and sacrament and the Methodist distinctive of itinerant ministry within the covenant of conference membership. The Order of Elder is closely aligned with the ecumenical consensus that calls for ordaining presbyters to Word and Sacrament, but includes the uniquely Methodist ordination to "Order." The inclusion of Service calls the elder to ministry in the world, not confined to the sanctuary or the chancel. The distinct ministry of the elder is, however, somewhat compromised by the broader use of unordained clergy to carry out all the functions of the ordained elder during probation. Our allegiance to the historic conviction that there should be no sacramental administration without ordination becomes even more tenuous with this new ordering of ministry.

The linkage between conference membership and itineracy is one of our most important links with our history and a characteristic mark of the Methodist movement. The actions of the 1996 General Conference have the potential to change radically our understanding of both terms by disconnecting itineracy from conference membership. We now have conference members who are not itinerant and do not have the assurance of annual appointment within the conference. I believe itineracy has demonstrated its flexibility and adaptability through the many changes it has endured. If these changes create more effective ways of sending persons in service for the Church and expanding our outreach in the world in the name of Christ, they will be simply the latest in a variety of modifications in itineracy since the days of Wesley. But if the office of a non-itinerant deacon attracts not only persons called to service, but also some who choose it simply because they prefer not to be itinerant, the unique ministry of the deacon could be negated and our ability to provide pastoral leadership to every church undermined. We have yet to see the impact of this radical break with our roots.

The clergy session of the annual conference has also been broadened to allow laity on the Board of Ordained Ministry to vote on matters of ordination and clergy character. This holds the potential for a creative modeling of partnership in ministry and for building stronger ties between the various forms of ministry in the Church. It means, however, that the clergy session is no longer the covenant community of those who are under orders, but a representative session of the annual conference. Therefore, I have great hope in the creation of Orders as a possible vehicle to recover the distinctively Methodist notion of clergy gathered in community, nurturing each other and supporting each other in ministry.

As we shape ministry under the new ordering and as the new ordering shapes us, I believe that the basic issue of how to link current practice with our history should be an important part of the discussion.

The Sacramental Ministry

As we have seen, the need for sacraments and the conviction that there could be no sacramental administration without proper ordination was the driving force behind John Wesley's decision to ordain clergy for the church in America and remained constant for our first century. However, in more recent years the connection between sacraments and ordination has been weakened by the use of non-ordained persons (licensed local pastors) to celebrate the sacraments and now by the creation of an ordained ministry (the deacon in full connection) with no sacramental

146

authority. My expectation is that both of these realities are here to stay. Our tradition of pragmatic concerns about ministry taking precedence over theological or historical consistency is likely to continue. Local pastors will continue to be an important part of our pastoral ministry, and their role will expand as probationary members serve under a license. The current office of deacon in full connection is intended to be something different from the former deacon or the elder, and it is at the point of sacramental administration that this distinction is most evident. To discontinue the sacramental ministry of the local pastor or to grant sacramental authority to the deacon in full connection would only further confuse the situation.

In consideration of the sacraments, discussion of our ecumenical relations becomes significant. Recent statements from the Consultation on Church Union (COCU; Church of Christ Uniting) call for the full reconciliation of ministries, so that there might be "one ministry in Jesus Christ in relation to all." These conversations will require that United Methodists understand their own ordering of ministry if we are to discuss with others the issues of ordination and recognition of ministry with honesty and integrity.

I believe that we must acknowledge that we have defined ordination in a significantly different way from the understanding of Wesley, Asbury, Otterbein, and the Anglican tradition and our ecumenical partners. In the creation of the act of commissioning we have established a uniquely United Methodist liturgical act that is unknown to our ecumenical partners. The historic link between ordination and sacrament in United Methodism remains in the ministry of the elder, but no longer can be seen as a primary definition of all ordination. I believe all these changes will raise serious questions about what it means to grant mutual recognition of orders in the COCU dialogue. It very well could be that mutual recognition will mean nothing more than acknowledging each other's forms and orders as valid expressions of Christ's ministry with no genuine attempt to reconcile our various orders or to make them compatible or corresponding in form and meaning. As United Methodists we claim our freedom to order our life in ways that best fulfill our mission.

Effectiveness in Fulfilling the Mission of Christ

A primary test of any ordering of ministry is its effectiveness in fulfilling the mission to which Jesus calls us to "go . . . and make disciples of all nations, baptizing them in the name of the Father and of the Son and of the Holy Spirit, and teaching them to observe everything that I have commanded you" (Matt 28:19-20); to be the body of Christ scattered in the world; and to carry out the servanthood of Christ in the world. This is true for any church polity, but it is particularly characteristic of Methodism since from our very beginning the success of the movement has been measured by our effectiveness in fulfilling the evangelistic task. "It is often said of Methodism," writes Dennis Campbell, "that pragmatic concerns of ministry take priority over fine points of theology. In a sense this is true, but it is important to understand that there is a theological reason for the priority, namely evangelical mission."[2]

As a reform movement within the Church of England, the primary criterion for judging every aspect was Methodism's evangelical witness. John Wesley followed George Whitefield's model of field preaching with great hesitation until he determined that it was an effective tool for communicating the gospel. Once he was convinced of its value, this well-bred, highly educated Anglican priest found himself in the coal fields and on the street corners preaching the Word of God and encouraged his followers to do the same. It was completely contrary to his background and personality, but it worked! The same was true for his use of the class meetings, new forms of hymnody, and even ordinations for America. He was focused on the mission, and though Anglican tradition, liturgy, and polity were central to his ecclesiology, he was willing to adapt all of it in order to fulfill the evangelistic task. Francis Asbury, when called to defend his episcopacy and the work of the Methodists, pointed to their success in proclaiming the gospel. With the same willingness to adapt, Otterbein melded his German Reformed roots with other traditions in the early American context to carry on the revival.

The priority of effectiveness in fulfilling the mission is reflected in two of the "Questions for Examiners" asked of every candidate from the days of Wesley and Asbury until today: "Have they fruit? Have any been truly convinced of sin and converted to God, and are believers edified by their service?" (¶ 305.3). As we live into a new ordering of ministry, we must evaluate our new forms in light of these missional criteria.

This pragmatism has been our strength and sometimes our weakness. It has enabled us to move with the frontier, to adapt to changes in society, to transcend ethnic and cultural differences, and to mold our life in ways that meet the needs of the world. At times, however, it has also spawned a willingness to do whatever seems expedient at the moment rather than to seriously consider either our roots in the past or the implications for the future. In terms of ordination, Dennis Campbell points to our origins as an evangelistic movement as being a primary influence on our understanding of ministry. He acknowledges that Methodism has emphasized the priority of mission, even at the expense of theology:

> What happened was that the theology and practice of ordination was displaced by another aspect of the tradition, namely the priority of mission, and particularly that aspect of mission which was the highest priority for nineteenth century Methodism, evangelism. The major work of the early American Methodist preacher was evangelism. The chief end of preaching was conversion and the church grew rapidly. Sacramental ministries, pastoral care, teaching and administration all were subordinate to evangelism. Ordination seemed almost incidental. . . . Ordination came to mean little more than authorization for ministry and full membership in the annual conference. . . . The integrity of ordination was undercut because the fine points of theology were not determinative for American Methodists.[3]

What was determinative was the desire to effectively carry out the evangelistic task, the mission of the people called Methodist to proclaim the gospel in the tradition of John Wesley.

If the new ordering of ministry is to effectively fulfill the Church's mission, there must be a common understanding of the purpose of ordination and its relationship to that mission. An excellent statement of the mission of the Church was unfortunately lost in the 1992 revision of *The United Methodist Hymnal.* It comes from the "Order for Confirmation and Reception into the Church" in the 1964 hymnal:

> Dearly beloved, the Church is of God, and will be preserved to the end of time, for the conduct of worship and the due administration of his Word and Sacraments, the maintenance of Christian fellowship and discipline, the edification of believers, and the conversion of the world.[4]

Today as Methodism struggles to articulate and claim a common mission, the evangelistic task should still be the driving force. In defining the mission of the church, the *Book of Discipline* clearly states that "the mission of the church is to make disciples of Jesus Christ by proclaiming the good news of God's grace and thus seeking the fulfillment of God's reign and realm in the world. . . . Whenever United Methodism has had a clear sense of mission, God has used our Church to save persons, heal relationships, transform social structures, and spread scriptural holiness, thereby changing the world. In order to be truly alive, we embrace Jesus' mandate to make disciples of all peoples" (¶ 200).

The *Discipline* discusses the meaning of ministry in its various forms and concludes:

> Beyond the diverse forms of ministry is this ultimate concern: that all persons will be brought into a saving relationship with God through Jesus Christ and be renewed after the image of their Creator. This means that all Christians are called to minister wherever Christ would have them serve and witness in deeds and words that heal and free. (¶ 105)

> The people of God, who are the church made visible in the world, must convince the world of the reality of the gospel or leave it unconvinced. There can be no evasion or delegation of this responsibility; the church is either faithful as a witnessing and serving community, or it loses its vitality and its impact on an unbelieving world. (¶ 107)

150

In relation to this mission, United Methodist ordination sets apart persons called by God for leadership in this evangelistic task. Given that both deacon and elder are ordained to Word, there is hope that these Orders of ministry will continue the Wesleyan vision for communicating the gospel to the end that, in the words of Charles Wesley, "all might catch the flame, All partake the glorious bliss."[5]

In this light, it is important to note the focus of the 1996 legislation on service as the "primary form of [Jesus'] ministry in God's name" (¶ 310) and the terminology of servant ministry and servant leadership in chapter 6 of the *Discipline* and following. In evaluating the new ordering of ministry, one must ask if this emphasis on the servanthood of the Church compels us to more effective witness in the world in the name of Christ. If so, it is to be celebrated. If we can once again embody the passion of the early Methodists for prison reform, education, abolition, and social ministry, we could see another rise of Methodism and a renewed society. But if this focus on service contributes to a weakening of Methodism's historic commitment to the evangelistic task, we will have lost the reason for our existence. If it contributes to more effective witness for Jesus Christ by laypersons and clergy alike, it will be only the latest example of Methodism's pragmatic response to our missional mandate. It is crucial that all ordained ministers, both deacons and elders, "make a commitment to conscious living of the whole gospel and to the proclamation of that gospel to the end that the world may be saved" (¶ 303).

Conclusion

Given that we have only just begun to live into this new structuring, it is too early to know its full impact. We have yet to see candidates come through the process for ordination as deacon who were not formerly diaconal ministers, to see how the new process shapes their ministry and how their presence impacts the whole. If they bring a new focus on service and effectively lead all baptized Christians into broader witness and service beyond the church walls in the same way the Holy Club and the Class Meeting touched the prisoner and the outcast, we could see a new Wesleyan revival.

We have yet to see candidates for ordination as elder who have not been first ordained deacon. If this new ordering of ministry leads them to a clearer understanding of their distinct identity as elders and creates a more holistic approach to the ministry of Service, Word, Sacrament, and Order, their leadership in the church will be strengthened. But if, on the other hand, the elder is seen solely as a sacradotal priest and the ministry is narrowed to parish maintenance, we could significantly weaken the leadership role of the elder in the fullness of ministry and mission.

We have yet to see how the presence of two ordained ministries, one itinerant and one non-itinerant, will effect the appointment system and our historic commitment to itinerant ministry. If we can discover a new sense of mission and a passion for proclaiming the gospel, we might bring new vitality to itineracy. But if conference membership and itineracy deteriorate into nothing more than benefits, voting rights, and tenure, the dynamic force of Methodism will be lost.

The presence of clergy members with three very different covenants of membership (deacons, elders, and local pastors) and laity members of the Board of Ordained Ministry will reshape the clergy session. If this broader membership in the clergy session strengthens the sense of partnership in ministry, it will be a healthy step. However, if it dilutes the accountability and covenant inherent in the ordering of ministry by weakening the sense of mutual oversight and shared vows, it could contribute to an unhealthy shift in clergy covenant and to even further malaise. We are full of hope that the creation of Orders for deacons and elders will provide the urgently needed community of vocation and spiritual renewal and help to address the spiritual hunger in the lives of clergy, so that they can more effectively lead the spiritual life of their congregations. If they become nothing more than special-interest caucus groups lobbying for the rights and concerns of their members, it will create animosity and division within the ranks of the clergy and between clergy and laity.

All these and more questions await answers that can only be discerned in practice. We are called, in the words of Charles Wesley,

> *To serve the present age, my calling to fulfill;*
> *O may it all my powers engage to do my Master's will.*[6]

As we live into the future with newly ordered ministry, the calling remains the same and the world awaits our witness in the name of the living Christ.

Appendixes

Appendix 1. Services for the Ordering of Ministry

From *Services for the Ordering of Ministry in The United Methodist Church: Provisional Texts,* March 1, 1998.

A. Commissioning and Ordination

Acts of ordination and commissioning, as well as consecrating and certifying, are anchored in the sacrament of baptism and the ministry of the baptized. These sign-acts are based on what is already implicit in baptism and rest upon the essential ministry given to all Christians in baptism. "By Water and the Spirit: A United Methodist Understanding of Baptism" states, "Through baptism, God calls and commissions persons to the general ministry of all Christian believers" (*The Book of Resolutions*—1996, p. 732). The paper goes on to say, "The vocation of those in representative [consecrated and ordained] ministry includes focusing, modeling, supervising, shepherding, enabling, and empowering the general ministry of the Church . . . [and] is grounded in the same baptism that commissions the general priesthood of all believers" (p. 733).

1. Commissioning

By the prompting of the Spirit, the church has always "sent" persons in various forms of ministry and mission, generally for specific service as missionaries, work team members, and certified workers in specialized ministries. One aspect distinguishing the commissioning of probationary members from ordination of elders and deacons is duration: commissioning sends persons to a term of service, while ordination sets persons apart for lifelong service.

Commissioning may be compared to the experience of the early church in Antioch when the Holy Spirit instructed the community to "set apart Barnabas and Saul for the work to which I have called them" (Acts 13). The probationary period and the mentoring relationship that characterize it can also be seen in light of the relationship of Paul and Ananias (Acts 9) when the newly called evangelist was guided toward the fullness of his calling by the more seasoned leader.

The act of commissioning probationary members
- Acknowledges and affirms God's call and the candidates' response, gifts, abilities, and training for servant leadership
- Invokes God's grace for true service
- Credentials candidates to lead the church and equip others for ministry
- Calls candidates to enter a time of evaluation of their effectiveness for lifelong service as ordained ministers
- Offers candidates the support of the annual conference

The qualifications for election to probationary membership and commissioning include: two years of candidacy; two years in a service setting; meeting the necessary educational requirements; presenting a health report; completing a written and oral examination; securing recommendations from the district committee and conference board of ordained ministry; having a favorable record in relation to felony, misdemeanor, or any incident of sexual misconduct; and submitting a written autobiographical statement. Upon recommendation of the conference board of ordained ministry and election to probationary membership by the annual conference, the commissioning may take place. See *The Book of Discipline—1996*, ¶ 315.1-13.

Those commissioned are to be appointed by the bishop to serve a minimum of three years as probationary members. The expectation of the three years of service includes: participation in theological growth using covenant groups to support their practice and work in servant leadership; contemplation of the grounding of ordained ministry and formation in covenant ministry in the annual conference; evaluation in terms of their ability to express and give leadership in servant ministry; engagement in ministries related to the order to which they plan to give themselves (those intending a lifetime as deacons in ministries of Word and Service and those intending a lifetime as elders in ministries of Service, Word, Sacrament, and Order). During this period of anticipating full connection, the commissioned are on probation as to character, servant leadership, and effectiveness in ministry. See *The Book of Discipline—1996,* ¶ 317.1-2.

The creation of the new category of Commissioned Ministers relates persons to the annual conference and to the ministry of the probationary members within the annual conference. Commissioning implies that the person is being "sent" by the annual conference for service and the annual conference invokes the Holy Spirit to empower commissioned ministers during their time of probationary membership. The probationary period is a time of full service and a temporary stage in one's journey toward ordination and full membership in the annual conference.

During probation, if a person is to serve as a pastor in a local church, he or she will be authorized for sacramental and pastoral duties through a local pastor's license. See the *Discipline—1996,* ¶ 341.

The period of commissioned ministry is concluded when the person is received as a full member of the annual conference and ordained as a deacon or elder, or as a decision is made not to proceed toward ordination.

2. Ordination

Anchored in the baptismal call to live lives of love, justice, and service, there are some Christians whose "gifts, evidence of God's grace, and promise of future usefulness are affirmed by the community and who respond to God's call by offering themselves in leadership as ordained ministers" (1996 *Book of Discipline*, ¶ 301.2).

Ordination is chiefly understood as the act of the Holy Spirit. It is the Spirit's call that makes one a minister, lay or clergy. As a liturgical act, ordination is also understood as the public prayer of the church confirming the Spirit's call to individuals and asking for them gifts and power for the ministry of deacon or elder in the church.

The rite of ordination is the climax of a process in which the faith community discerns and validates the call, the gifts, and effectiveness for apostolic ministry by agency of the Holy Spirit. This is a full process in which all of the baptized share; it is not to be confined to one sacramental moment. The process begins with the church's discernment of God's call to individuals for service as ordained leaders, continues with support and scrutiny as they prepare for this work, culminates in electing them to the office and work of a deacon or elder, and is celebrated and enacted liturgically in the service of ordination.

The liturgical structure and action in the rite of ordination include: recognition of our common ministry; presentation of those called to be set apart for apostolic ministry; the proclamation of the Word of God in light of the occasion; examination of the candidates; prayer for the grace of God to fortify and equip them for the office and work to which they are to be ordained by invocation of the Holy Spirit with the laying on of hands; authorization to do the work of the Order to which the candidates are ordained; and celebration of the Eucharist.

Ordination is both to an office and a work for a lifetime. Ordination confers a new identity as well as authority for ministry. The new identity is always claimed in relation to Christ and his call to leadership and service of the baptized for the life of the world. The authority is always exercised in stewardship of the mysteries of the gospel and the church's mission in the world.

Ordination has to do with who the person is as well as what the person does in ministry. Through ordination one becomes a clergy person and assumes a new identity in the church and in the world.

Upon ordination, ordained persons become accountable to the whole church, the community of the ordained, and to the Order. In the rite of ordination, ordinands express loyalty to The United Methodist Church, accepting its order, liturgy, doctrine, and discipline; accept the responsibility of accountability to the bishop and to the annual conference; and are charged with authority for appointment to their places of service.

B. The Laying on of Hands

The laying on of hands with prayer by the bishop is an ancient and essential part of the Christian ordering of ministry. This action, however, must always be seen in its larger context. The ordination service as a whole emphasizes the prayer of the whole church. This emphasis does not undermine the importance of the laying on of hands with prayer by the bishop, but makes clear that such a prayer and gesture always take place in the context of the assembled community's life and liturgy. Further, the emphasis makes clear that ordained ministry is formed and belongs within the ministry of the whole church.

The laying on of hands is not to be confused with the grace of ordination itself. The bestowal of this grace is the action of the Holy Spirit in the life of the ordinand, but the church prays for this action of the Spirit through the laying on of hands and recognizes the Spirit's power at work in those who have received this sign-act. The connection through the physical touch between the ordinand and those who participate in the laying on of hands establishes the real connection between those who share in ordained ministry and symbolically connects the ordinand to all those who have shared in this ministry in all ages.

The laying on of hands is a part of the act of prayer in ordination, as the touching and lifting of the eucharistic elements are part of the eucharistic prayer. It is essential that there be clarity about the meaning of the laying on of hands with prayer. It is more than a way of saying, "I concur with this action of ordaining this person for ministry." That has been done already, in the prior approval by the charge conference, in the examination by the district and conference committees on ordained ministry, and in the election of the candidates by the clergy session of the annual conference. It is more than a way of saying, "I offer my love and support to this person at the point of his or her ordination." That may be done in other ways and at other points within or outside of the rite. The laying on of hands is the invoking of the Spirit for the office and work to which God has called the person.

Who is permitted to pray the spoken ordination prayer? The bishop, as the presiding minister in the annual conference and as a general superintendent of the whole church, speaks the words, and the congregation joins in prayer through the bishop's leadership. This presidential action focuses the prayer of all and connects the assembled community's invocation of the Holy Spirit for each ordinand.

Who joins prayer by participating in the laying on of hands? The historic practice has been for the bishop alone to lay hands on those being ordained deacon and the bishop assisted by elders to lay hands on those being ordained elders. This practice has been rooted in a historic understanding of the relationship of each order to the bishop; deacons as persons assisting the bishop directly in works of charity and administration and elders as persons assisting the bishop in presiding at the Eucharist and in guiding communal life. This tradition dates from a time when elders and deacons were truly separate orders of ministry with distinct roles in the life of the church.

The 1996 General Conference both affirmed the church's historic orders and expressed its clear intention that these orders be distinct and equal. Consequently, the revised services of ordination are shaped by these understandings with respect to the laying on of hands:

- The General Conference created distinct orders of ministry, which are different in office and work, but it clearly intended for them to be equal orders in leading the church in its mission and ministry.

- This new ordering of ministry recovers the fullness of the relationship among deacons, elders, and bishops.
- The appropriate way to recognize the equality of the distinctive orders is for both orders to play a collegial role in ordination of persons to their respective orders.

The collegial pattern that the tradition has long observed in the ordination of elders is appropriate for United Methodist ordination to both orders of clergy. Thus the bishop, as the presiding officer of the annual conference and general superintendent, leads the elders in laying hands on those who are to be ordained elders and leads deacons in laying hands on those who are to be ordained deacon in full connection.

Two additional concerns related to the issue of who joins in the laying on of hands:

First, since ordination is an act of the whole church invoking the Holy Spirit and giving authority to the ordinands, the participation of any Christian in the laying on of hands cannot be ruled out on principle. The question here is one of good order. To maintain an appearance appropriate to the unity of the United Methodist ministry, practices (1) should not vary widely from place to place, and (2) should adhere to the limits imposed by decorum and efficiency—not principled restriction on participation related to the laying on of hands. Although the *Discipline* offers to bishops wide discretion regarding participation in the laying on of hands, these provisional texts urge simplicity and uniformity in practice, so that the liturgical action is clear, visible, and not unduly long.

Based on the argument that the laying on of hands in a United Methodist rite of ordination should always include, in addition to the ordaining bishop, the participation of others who share the order into which the ordinand is being ordained, the multiplication of colleagues in the order to which the candidates are ordained poses no problem in principle. Good order and simplicity will guide the bishop in deciding the number who share in the laying on of hands.

Bishops of other traditions and ecumenical representatives with ordaining authority may, at the discretion of the presiding bishop, join in laying hands on those being ordained. Such participation is strongly recommended and is a faithful witness to United Methodist ecumenical commitments. The resident bishop and planners will need to factor the participation of ecumenical representatives into the number of persons who will share in the laying on of hands.

Second, the question of good order guides the bishop in deciding whether or not persons who do not share the order into which the ordinands are being ordained should participate in the laying on of hands. Great care must be taken to avoid conveying the impression that these persons are providing an endorsement of the ordinand, or that they participate in the laying on of hands as representatives of the whole church. Endorsements are provided at the presentation of the candidates at the beginning of the service. The whole church is present in the prayer of the presiding bishop. Whatever purposes the participation of others in the laying on of hands may serve, it cannot be that they would otherwise not participate in the ordination. For this reason, configurations that aim to include elders, deacons, non-ordained persons, and ecumenical guests in an attempt to achieve comprehensive, representative participation in the laying on of hands are particularly to be avoided.

In summary, the logic of the distinctive and equal order of deacons and elders in The United Methodist Church implies a normative ordination action in which the presiding bishop, as part of the prayer offered verbally on behalf of all Christians, joins with deacons or elders to lay hands on the ordinands; deacons with deacon ordinands, and elders with elder ordinands. Other participants are not ruled out on principle, but it should be avoided in the interest of good order, especially where the number and variety of participants may obscure the presiding role of the bishop and representative clergy of the order into which a person is being ordained.

C. The Ordination Prayer, the Laying on of Hands, and the Charge

Historically, the ordination prayer is a single prayer that includes the moment when hands are laid upon each ordinand. The unity of this prayer is observable and heard as one prayer in circumstances where only one person is ordained a deacon or an elder. Since United Methodist polity and practice require the election and ordination during the sessions of the annual conference of all persons taking orders, the numbers of ordinands involved make it difficult to portray the unity of the prayer and to keep the duration of the service within acceptable limits.

The liturgy as a whole provides ways for all of the congregation to participate. For this reason, actions and gestures showing support, endorsement, or welcome of the ordinands by family, friends, and mentoring or sponsoring clergy need not be expressed at the moment of ordination prayer with the laying on of hands.

Simplicity is essential so that the flow of the prayer can be experienced and expressed with clarity. This is particularly true when it involves the movement of people for the laying on of hands. In many cases, the movement of the bishop from ordinand to ordinand for the laying on of hands may be logistically simpler than movement of ordinands to the bishop. Utmost care in planning for simplicity is imperative.

As an accommodation to the particular cicumstances in each annual conference's number of ordinands and the worship space where ordinantions will take place, the rubrics for the prayer in these services provide the option of excising the specific invocation of the Holy Spirit ("Lord, pour upon *name* the Holy Spirit . . . ") to come immediately after the prayer and to be followed with the charge to each ordinand, *"Name,* take thou authority . . . "

This eliminates a double movement of the bishop to each ordinand.

162

Appendix 2. Ministry Interpretation Materials—1997

Clergy Members and the Clergy Session

"1. Ministry in the Christian church is derived from the ministry of Christ, who calls all persons to receive God's gift of salvation and follow in the way of love and service. The whole church receives and accepts this call, and all Christians participate in this continuing ministry (see ¶¶ 101-117). 2. Within the church community, there are persons whose gifts, evidence of God's grace, and promise of future usefulness are affirmed by the community, and who respond to God's call by offering themselves in leadership as ordained ministers." (¶ 301)

Ordained ministers are called to a lifetime of servant leadership in specialized ministries among the people of God. (¶ 116)

There shall be an annual meeting of this covenant body in executive session of clergy members in full connection. (¶ 324)*

The ordering of ministry by the 1996 General Conference gives a new definition of clergy: *"Clergy* in The United Methodist Church are individuals who serve as commissioned ministers, deacons, elders, and local pastors under appointment of a bishop (full- and part-time), who hold membership in an annual conference, and who are commissioned, ordained, or licensed" (¶ 119). All clergy are members of the annual conference and have voice and vote in the annual conference session. Only clergy members in full connection can vote for and be elected as ministerial delegates to General and jurisdictional conferences as defined in ¶ 33 of the 1996 *Book of Discipline.*

The clergy session deals with all matters of ordination, character, and conference relations of clergy on behalf of the annual

* All paragraph references refer to *The Book of Discipline—1996.*

conference. All clergy members of the conference and lay members of the board of ordained ministry may attend and have voice in the clergy session. Only elders and deacons in full connection and lay members of the board of ordained ministry may vote (¶¶ 605.6; 320.2; 324; and 325.1).

This action creates a new covenant community of all who are identified as clergy and gives laity direct voice in clergy matters. The composition of the clergy session has changed, but the important task of approving and supporting clergy who will give effective leadership for the future continues with an intense fervor! It is a new clergy session which will convene in 1997, bringing together all who "live with all other ordained ministers in mutual trust and concern and seek with them the sanctification of the fellowship" (¶ 324).

The Ordained Deacon in Full Connection

Those who respond to God's call to lead in service and to equip others for this ministry through teaching, proclamation, and worship and who assist elders in the administration of the sacraments and are ordained deacons. (¶ 303.2)

1. Ordained to Word and Service

Deacons are persons called by God, authorized by the church, and ordained by a bishop to a lifetime ministry of Word and Service to both the community and the congregation in a ministry that connects the two. Deacons exemplify Christian discipleship and create opportunities for others to enter into discipleship, and connect the needs and hurts of the people with the church: in the world, where the deacon seeks to express a ministry of compassion and justice and assists lay persons as they claim their own ministry; and in the congregation where the ministry of the deacon is to teach and to form disciples, and to lead worship together with other ordained and lay persons (connecting the needs and hurts of the people with the church).

Deacons give leadership in the church's life: in the teaching and proclamation of the word; in worship and in assisting the elders in the administration of the Sacraments of Baptism and the Lord's Supper; in the congregation's mission to the world; and in leading the congregation in interpreting the needs, concerns, and hopes of the world (¶ 320).

2. Called and set apart for a ministry of service

From the earliest days of the church, deacons were called and set apart for the ministry of love, justice, and service; of connecting the church with the most needy, neglected, and marginalized among the children of God. This ministry grows out of the Wesleyan passion for social holiness and ministry among the poor. . . . the ministry of the deacon is a faithful response of the mission of the Church meeting the emerging needs of the future. Deacons are accountable to the annual conference and the bishop for the fulfillment of their call to servant leadership (¶ 319).

3. Appointment

Deacons may be appointed through agencies and settings beyond the local church that extend the witness and service of Christ in the world; through The United Methodist Church related agencies, schools, colleges, theological schools, and ecumenical agencies; and within a local congregation, charge or cooperative parish (¶ 322.1) and will be non-itinerate. If a deacon is appointed beyond the local church he/she will also be appointed to a local church (¶ 322.2).

The deacon is defined as an office of service ministry distinct and apart from the ministry of the elder. Although it is possible for the deacon to be licensed as a local pastor, this is not the vocational calling or training of the new deacon and should only be done in exceptional circumstances for missional purposes and for a particular time.

Deacons in full connection are clergy members and shall have voice and vote in the clergy session and the annual conference where membership is held.

The Ordained Elder in Full Connection

Those whose leadership in service includes preaching and teaching the Word of God, administration of the sacraments, ordering the Church for its mission and service, and administration of the Discipline *of the Church are ordained as elders.* (¶ 303.2)

1. Ordained to Word, Sacrament, and Order

The elder shares with the deacon responsibility for "Word," the apostolic task of the faithful transmission of the faith and proclamation of the Word of God. For the elder, this includes primary responsibility for the preaching ministry, though preaching in Methodism has always included the lay preacher as well as the ordained. The unique focus of the elder is the responsibility for administration of the sacraments and the ordering of the ministry of the church. For most elders, this will be lived out as the pastor in charge of a local congregation, but the elder's ministry is not restricted to the parish. They may be appointed to "extension ministries" (¶ 334), serving in a variety of settings. Because elders have been ordained to ordering the ministry of the church and administering the *Discipline,* bishops and district superintendents are chosen from the ordained elders. Elders share with the bishop the responsibility for this ministry and serve as pastors in charge in the congregation.

2. Ordained to service

With the deacon, the elder is ordained to service. The addition of the word "service" to the elder's ordination is important, since all ordained ministry is rooted in servant leadership. Since the elder will no longer be ordained deacon, this makes clear that there is a diaconal aspect to the ministry of the elder, lest elders be narrowly defined as parish priests within the congregation. For Wesley this meant refusing the constraints of parish boundaries and claiming the world as his parish. For us it means that elders as well as deacons are responsible for leading the church in service in the world. The elder is specifically ordained to "order the church for its mission and service."

166

3. Itinerant clergy

The elder continues to be itinerant, offering him/her self "without reserve to be appointed and to serve" where needed for the sake of the mission of the church (¶ 324). The traveling elder commits him/herself to full-time service in the connection under the authority of the bishop. All elders who are in good standing shall be continued under appointment unless they are on leave and are assured equitable compensation for their ministry (¶ 333).

4. Elder as pastor-in-charge

As pastor of a local congregation, the elder assumes responsibility to "oversee the total ministry of the local church in its nurturing ministries and in fulfilling its mission of witness and service in the world." These responsibilities are outlined in ¶ 331.

The Local Pastor

A local pastor is approved and licensed to perform the duties of a pastor while appointed to a particular charge. All persons not ordained as elders who are appointed to preach and conduct divine worship and perform the duties of a pastor shall have a license as a local pastor (¶¶ 340-341).

1. The essential ministry of the local pastor

Essential to the ministry of early Methodism was the lay preacher, the exhorter, the class leader. These persons, though not ordained, provided primary forms of ministry and leadership in the frontier church. That ministry is continued through the local pastor. Though not ordained, the local pastor is authorized to provide pastoral leadership to the local church, including sacramental administration and the responsibility to order the mission and ministry of the congregation. Full-time and part-time local pastors have vote as clergy members of the annual conference and have voice in the clergy session.

2. Categories of local pastors (¶ 343)

- *Full-time local pastors*
  Full-time local pastors devote their entire time to the charge to which they are appointed and its outreach in ministry and mission to the community. They must complete the course of study program and have their license renewed annually.

- *Part-time local pastors*
  Lay persons who have met the provisions of the *Discipline* and do not devote their entire time to the charge may be appointed as part-time local pastors. They must complete at least two courses per year in the course of study.

- *Student local pastors*
  Those enrolled in colleges, universities or schools of theology and who are making progress in their education may be licensed as a student local pastor.

- *Associate Members*
  Local pastors who have made progress toward associate minister may continue their preparation and be received as an associate member under the provisions of the 1992 *Book of Discipline,* depending upon the policies of the annual conference board of ordained ministry.

3. Local pastor as pastor-in-charge

As pastor of a local church, the local pastor assumes the full responsibilities of the pastor (¶ 331). He/she is licensed to serve in that appointment under the direct supervision of the district superintendent. A local pastor may only serve in appointment to a local church.

The Ordained Deacon and Elder in Appointments Extending the Ministry of Christ

Elders in effective relationship may be appointed to serve in ministry settings beyond the local United Methodist church in the witness and service of Christ's love and justice. (¶ 334.1)

Deacons in full connection may be appointed to serve in various ministries beyond the local church. (¶ 322.1)

1. Extending the ministry of Christ

Basic to our understanding of ministry is that all persons have the right to receive the full ministry of the gospel of Jesus Christ. Ministry is the responsibility of every Christian and extends to every place and to all persons through acts of love and service that convey God's love and the love of God's people. The full ministry of Christ extends beyond the congregation to persons in special situations or with special needs which require an interfaith outreach or ministry by persons with both a calling and specific qualifications for work in specialized settings. Both the ordained elder and deacon extend the ministry in particular ways.

2. The elder in extension ministries (¶¶ 334-336)

Extension Ministries, formerly called appointments beyond the local church, normally take place outside the boundaries of a local congregation. Extension ministries are initiated in missional response to the needs of persons in special circumstances and unique situations and may be time-limited as needs and situations change. Endorsement for some extension ministries, such as military chaplaincy, is carried out by the Section of Chaplains and Related Ministries of the General Board of Higher Education and Ministry (¶ 1411.2c).

Elders may be appointed to extension ministries in the following categories:

a. Within the connectional structures of United Methodism
b. Endorsed ministry settings
c. Under the General Board of Global Ministries
d. Ecumenical settings and ministries that are not usually provided for by the local church.

3. The deacon in various ministries (¶ 322)

By its very nature and vision, the deacon in full connection extends the ministry of Christ into the community. Whether a deacon's primary appointment is to a local congregation, denominational, ecumenical agency, or settings that extend the witness and service of Christ, they are compelled to serve the needs and hurts of the world as well as equip and call out members of the congregation to serve Christ in the world. All deacons are appointed to a local church regardless of their service setting and charged to interrelate the altar table and the marketplace.

Ministry settings that require endorsement may be filled by the deacon in full connection if sacramental authority is not required. Endorsement will be done by the Section of Chaplains and Related Ministries (¶ 1411.2c).

4. Fulfilling the ministry of Christ

These ministers represent God's new thing in a new time. John Wesley was a practitioner of "holy pragmatism," and made use of whatever strategies and structures that were useful to fulfill the mission for which God had raised up "the people called Methodist."

This kind of pragmatism has been characteristic of our Methodist tradition which has always been more mission oriented than churchly. Appointments that extend the ministry of Christ enable The United Methodist Church to demonstrate in concrete ways that the world is, indeed, our parish.

The Order of Deacons and the Order of Elders

There shall be in each annual conference an Order of Deacons and an Order of Elders. . . . a covenant community . . . to mutually support, care for, and hold accountable its members for the sake of the life and mission of the church. (¶ 311).

General Conference has now made possible a structure through which the vocation and covenant for elders and deacons in full conference membership can be affirmed. We have an opportunity for, indeed a calling into, covenant relationships with our colleagues. The Order will "seek to respond to the spiritual hunger among clergy for a fulfilling sense of vocation, for support among peers . . . and for a deepening relationship with God" (¶ 311). Each annual conference will have an Order of Elders and an Order of Deacons. The purpose is multi-dimensional, yet will include:

1. Providing regular gatherings for continuing formation in relationship to Jesus Christ through study of the Bible, church and societal issues, and theological exploration of vocation;
2. Assisting clergy in plans for individual study and retreat;
3. Developing a bond of commitment to mission and ministry of the UMC;
4. Fostering relationships of mutual accountability and trust; and,
5. Holding accountable each other in fulfilling these purposes (¶ 312).

It may be tempting to rush the process of enacting the legislation so that the Order of Elder and Order of Deacon are in place immediately. However, to hurry in the creation of these Orders is an antithesis of what the Order is about. The purpose is for conversation, exploration, prayer, and relationship. Each annual conference will need to engage in a process that makes the Order indigenous to the annual conference, to the identity of its members, and to welcome the full participation of clergy members.

The Order of Deacons and the Order of Elders may meet separately or together. The Orders are to be convened by the bishop. The chairperson is nominated by the board of ordained ministry and is elected by the full membership of the Order. Clergy are members of the Order by ordination and full membership in the annual conference.

Persons become members of the Order upon their ordination and election to full clergy membership in the annual conference.

Appendix 3. Dr. Robin Lovin's Letter to the Ordinal Working Group

Dr. Robin Lovin served as a resource to the Council of Bishops during the 1993–96 quadrennium as they conducted their study of the ministry. He worked closely with the writing and was present in the 1996 legislative committee sessions as the report was revised by that group. He has continued to be involved in the interpretation of the action of the General Conference and consulted with the Ordinal Revision Working Group. The following paper was presented to that committee and is directed at the many issues related to the development of a new ordinal. Many of those issues are not addressed in this paper. However, his reflections on the new ordering of ministry, and particularly the creation of the new office of deacon in full connection are insightful, given his role as a scholar, participant and observer in the process. I share an edited version of his paper, focusing on these issues rather than the details of the proposed ordinal.

Ordinal Revision Working Group
General Board of Discipleship
The United Methodist Church

Dear Colleagues:

Thanks very much for the opportunity to comment on the proposed ordinal revision. I realize that we are all working under time constraints (the GBOD and GBHEM staff have been heroic in their efforts to translate the actions of the General Conference on ministry into working guidelines for the bishops and annual conferences—so I will offer these preliminary reflections, without attempting the detailed response that your work deserves. I have three general thoughts.

First, the ordained deacon given us by General Conference is an order of clergy quite different from the "transitional" deacon of the Methodist tradition or the diaconate of the Anglo-Catholic tradition. The new deacon is in organic relationship to the whole body of Christ's people, but the office as established by General Conference resists the usual ways of relating it to the ministry of the bishop or the elders. In particular, the traditional liturgical role of the deacon is suppressed in favor of a ministry of service that is primarily related to the work of Christ's people in the world, rather than to the ordered relationships symbolized in the arrangement of the ministers around the Lord's Table. It is, of course, the intent of the new ordering of ministry that the deacon shall relate "the altar and the marketplace," or in the good words of the proposed ordinal, "interpret to the Church the hurts and hopes of the world." But I find it hard to believe that those who conceived the work of the deacon in such radical independence from that of the elder will be happy with the role of servant and assistant that is acted out in the proposed ordinal, taken as it is from a tradition of the deacon's ministry that was largely rejected in the conceptualization of the new order of deacon.

The traditional relationship between the deacons and the bishop, likewise, seems inappropriate to the new United Methodist office. In our ordering of ministry, it is the elders, not the deacons, who will occupy the traditional place of the deacon as those who perform their ministry under the direction and supervision of the bishop. The deacons will, necessarily, be more directly dependent on those persons (sometimes elders, sometimes not) who supervise their work in their place of ministry. It is important to remember that when the new ordering of ministry is fully implemented, the bishop who ordains the deacons will not be an ordained deacon.

In short, I find it easier to understand the ordering of ministry passed by the General Conference as involving the creation of a new order of ordained minister for which today's church has borrowed the ancient title of "deacon." This is quite a normal pattern of development in the history of the church, and appropriate to the great range of service ministries to which the name of deacon has historically been given. It is likewise appropriate for those attempting to understand this new office to reach back into history for traditions and rituals to aid in the interpretation. But I find the effort of the proposed ordinal to apply the traditional Anglo-Catholic role and symbols of the deacon wholesale to this new office unconvincing.

The implication of this is, of course, a fairly radical critique of the proposed new ordinal as it relates to the deacon. I have a sense that we need to start over and ask what this new office is and what traditions (perhaps from a variety of uses of the title "deacon") are appropriate to it. I am less clear what the results would be if we did that.

A second major point concerns the commissioning of probationary members. It is imperative that both the church and the probationary members be clear that these persons are sent out as fully competent leaders of the Christian community, accountable to the same standards of diligence, competence, and integrity that apply to ordained elders and deacons. We must not imply to any congregation that they are there to give their appointed pastor a place to practice his or her skills, or space in which to explore his or her calling. Congregations and probationers alike must be clear about the difference between an "intern" or a "student pastor" and a leader in ministry who happens to be a probationary member of the Annual Conference. The move from ordaining these persons to commissioning them runs a risk of conveying the impression that they're not quite ready yet. Of course, we anticipate that persons grow in ministry through their whole lives, that in some sense we are never ready for this calling. And we know from experience that they grow a lot during the first few years of full-time ministry. That is what the new, extended probationary period is all about. But we also have to understand the import of the new requirement that no one is ready to be commissioned until he or she has completed the necessary education for his or her ministry and is ready to live out that ministry as a full-time, demanding vocation.

Let me make a third general observation about the theology of commissioning. On the whole, as I say, I think the service is clear about what we are doing, but at two points the language is a bit unusual, and I wonder if these word choices were deliberate: At the examination, the bishop inquires into the probationary members' "readiness for accepting this commission." After the examination, the bishop asks the people whether they are willing for these men and women to be commissioned. All this tends to make the commissioning seem rather more like a voluntary agreement between the people and the probationers, rather than an affirmation of God's claim on the probationers' lives and an acceptance by the people of their readiness and worthiness for the tasks they are about to undertake. On a worst-case analysis, the peoples' response, "We are willing," set alongside the affirmation of worthiness, "We do. Thanks be to God," in the elder's ordination simply underscores the preliminary and incomplete nature of probationary ministry. The line about "trusting the preparation and examination of those who have known and cared for them" which precedes the "We are willing," lends itself to an interpretation that this means, "OK, if you say so, we'll give it a go." Hardly the kind of endorsement with which to begin full-time ministry!

Thanks again for the hard work that went into this document. It's been very stimulating to respond to it, and I hope that the major issues I feel need to be raised will not obscure my admiration for the whole of the job that has been done.

Yours truly,

Robin Lovin, Dean
Perkins School of Theology
Southern Methodist University

Appendix 4. Bishops' Statement on Laying on of Hands, December 10, 1997

The Task Force on the Laying on of Hands in Ordination

The Task Force adopted some "Guiding Principles" to assist its work. There are presently at least seven "Guiding Principles," but more may be added if the task force so determines in subsequent meetings.

1. The historic tradition affirms the role of bishop as the ordainer through the laying on of hands; elders have been included to signify the "sealing of the ordination" in their order.
2. Developing consistence in the language of the *Discipline* re commissioning and ordination is important.
3. Laying on of hands has significance in many points in the faith journey of the individual and the community (e.g., baptism, confirmation, healing, commissioning of missionaries, ordination).
4. We affirm the ministry of all Christians as the basis for the ordering of our ministry; we further affirm the ordained ministry as servanthood equipping all persons for ministry to the world.
5. We desire to strengthen the ministry of all Christians through sign acts of ordination and other rituals to clarify what ministry is.
6. We acknowledge the paradoxes of our tradition (e.g., functioning of local pastors in sacramental and "ordering" roles); we will continue to have them.
7. New practices are evolving around our new understandings of and ordering of ministry.

At the meeting held on September 16-17, 1997, the Task Force agreed to the substance of the following statement:

177

We have examined the Tradition concerning the laying on of hands in ordination and believe we understand it. Our 1996 *Book of Discipline* provides for the bishop as the ordaining person in keeping with past history and tradition. When it speaks of the participation of others it makes the following dissimilar statements:

For deacon's orders, "The ordaining bishop may invite other elders, deacons, and laity to participate."

For elder's orders, "The ordaining bishop may invite other elders and laity to be a part of the laying on of hands."

We understand that the bishop is the ordaining person and in the case of elder's ordination that when other elders have been invited to participate in the laying on of hands it has been as an act of "sealing" or "confirming" the ordination. We affirm this practice.

Since annual conference sessions of 1997, we have full member deacons. This is historic because these ordinations were provided for by action of the 1996 General Conference. We believe that this is the time to create a new tradition in keeping with this decision. Bishops previous to this time have ordained deacons without the participation of the laying on of hands of other elders. In 1998, full member deacons are available to participate in the ordination of new deacons by the laying on of hands. We affirm the inviting of deacons to participate in the act of laying on of hands as a sealing or confirming of the ordination of the new deacon and as an act of "peer" participation of the entrance to the order. We do not affirm the involvement of elders in the laying on of hands in the ordaining of deacons.

We continue to study the issue of the involvement of laity in the laying on of hands.

William Dew
Chair of the Task Force

Appendix 5. Appointment of the Deacon

I. Appointment of Commissioned Ministers in Probation to be Ordained Deacons in Full Connection

The Book of Discipline of The United Methodist Church—1996

Among those who are commissioned ministers are clergy seeking to become ordained as deacon in full connection. The expectations for their participation in covenant peer groups, continuing theological education, clergy mentoring relationship and supervision by the district superintendent are parallel to the expectation for those seeking to be ordained as elders. They are on probation as to character, servant leadership, and effectiveness in ministry. They are reviewed and their relationship evaluated annually by the district superintendent and the board of ordained ministry. They may serve on any board, commission, or committee of the annual conference other than the board of ordained ministry. They are appointed annually by the bishop.

1. Commissioned ministers planning to give their lives as deacons in full connection shall be in ministries of service the entire probationary period. The annual conference may equate non-salaried service as meeting this qualification. Service is understood through the description of "The Ministry of a Deacon" (¶ 319).
2. Ministries of service by probationers are evaluated by the board of ordained ministry and laypersons directly involved in the commissioned minister's ministry as effective according to the boards written guidelines and adopted by the clergy session.
3. Commissioned ministers in settings of ministry beyond the local church are expected to be active in their local United Methodist church. Their setting is approved by the bishop and

cabinet. They do not receive a second appointment to a local church. Accountability is also provided by the employer.

4. Supervision is to be personally assumed or delegated by the district superintendent.

5. Mentoring is provided by a clergy mentor, preferably a deacon, assigned by the conference board of ordained ministry. The conference board may designate deacons in full connection for this role.

II. Appointment of Ordained Deacons in Full Connection

A. Appointment of a deacon to a local congregation, charge, or cooperative parish

1. The appointment may be initiated by the deacon, the bishop, the district superintendent, or the agency seeking their service. (¶ 322.4)

2. The position is clarified by a written statement of intentionality of servant leadership that makes the distinction between the work of all Christians and the work of the deacon. (¶ 322.4*b*)

3. It is recommended that a meeting be arranged with the pastor in charge and the staff-parish relations committee to consult on the appointment and, if acceptable, negotiate and clarify work expectations.

4. A joint letter (or form) of request for appointment is sent by the deacon and pastor to the bishop with a copy to the district superintendent. For deacons who are members of another conference the bishop communicates with the bishop of the deacon's home conference. If the bishop and cabinet consider an appointment not to be in the best interest of the church, the bishop may choose not to make the appointment (¶ 322.4*c*). Sites for ministry are not approved by the clergy session or conference board of ministry.

5. If the deacon is a member of another annual conference the bishop completes the "Official Record of Appointment of an

Ordained Deacon" (#251958 UMPH), signs and forwards it to the bishop in the home conference for the signature from that bishop.

6. Deacons complete an annual report for their charge conference, are evaluated annually by the staff-parish relations committee (¶ 262.2f4), and are appointed on an annual basis.

B. Appointment of a deacon beyond the local church

Primary appointment

1. The appointment may be initiated by the deacon, the bishop, the district superintendent, or the agency seeking their service (¶ 322.4a).
2. It is recommended a statement of request for serving in the setting beyond the local church be submitted by the deacon to the bishop with a copy to the district superintendent. The request is evaluated by the bishop and cabinet to determine the advisability and appropriateness of the appointment. Sites for ministry are not approved by the clergy session or conference board of ministry. Questions that may be raised are:

- Is the proposed ministry one in which the vows of ordination to Word and Service may be fulfilled?

- Does the setting provide opportunity to maintain a relationship and accountability with the order and structure of the church?

- Is the ministry congruent with the church's missional commitment in and to the world?

- Does the person posses the specific gifts, training, education and work experience for the proposed ministry?

- Is supervision provided in the setting with goals, evaluation and accountability acceptable to the bishop, cabinet, and the board of ordained ministry?

3. Special provisions are made for deacons whose primary appointment does not have accountability structures, but whose charge conference will supply this need (¶ 322.9). It is recommended that where this is not feasible a board of directors or an advisory committee be created by the deacon to provide accountability and guidance.

4. If the setting requires ecclesiastical endorsement, the deacon applies to the Section of Chaplains and Related Ministry, General Board of Higher Education and Ministry (¶ 344.9).

5. The position is clarified by a written statement of intentionality of servant leadership that makes the distinction between the work of all Christians and the work of the deacon. This is submitted by the deacon to the bishop and cabinet (¶ 322.4*b*).

6. The deacon's home conference bishop makes the primary appointment to church-related agencies. With the approval of their home bishop, deacons in other settings in other conferences may be appointed by the bishop of that conference. Form #251958 UMPH would be used to record the appointment.

Second appointment to a local church

1. An assignment to a local church is initiated by the bishop and/or district superintendent or by the deacon where an appointment is desired (¶ 322.4*a*).

2. The bishop in the episcopal area where the deacon is to be appointed shares the process with the cabinet, used in that annual conference. The suggested procedure is for the bishop with the district superintendent to give the deacon permission to initiate a conversation with the pastor in charge of the local church for a possible appointment (¶ 322.2). Following this conversation a consultation with the staff-parish relations committee is appropriate to get acquainted and explore the needs of the congregation.

3. The pastor in charge writes to the bishop and copies the district superintendent stating willingness in having the deacon appointed to the local church and the role of the deacon in that congregation.

4. If the deacon is a member of another annual conference the local bishop completes the "Official Record of Appointment of an Ordained Deacon" (#251958 UMPH) for the appointment to the local church, signs and forwards it to the bishop in the home conference for the signature from that bishop.
5. The deacon is accountable to the pastor in charge, the charge conference, and other bodies that coordinate the ministries of service.
6. Effectiveness shall be evaluated by the immediate supervisor in the context of the specific setting in which their primary ministry is performed. An annual report is made by the deacon to the charge conference in the second appointment.

Appendix 6. The Impact of General Conference 2000

Approaching the end of this first quadrennium under the new ordering of ministry, the Division of Ordained Ministry made an intentional decision to recommend no major changes in the legislation as adopted by the 1996 General Conference. In these four years the sixty-eight annual conference boards of ordained ministry and 550 district committees on ordained ministry reorganized their life to accommodate the changes enacted in 1996. Bishops and district superintendents sought to interpret this new understanding of ministry and adapt their practice to the changes in the appointive process. Central conferences considered the new concept of deacon and took the first steps to implement such an order in their context. The thirteen United Methodist seminaries have developed programs to meet the new educational requirements and have met with annual conference leaders to consider new models for probation. Yet, as noted in chapter 10, the church is only beginning to experience the impact of the dramatic changes of 1996. Given the need for time and experience to determine its effectiveness, the Division recommended and the General Conference adopted few changes in the legislation.

A. Commissioning

One change with theological as well as practical significance was the adoption of a new definition of commissioning. Following the work of the ordinal committee, the Division of Ordained Ministry proposed a definition based on the new ordinal, which was also adopted by the General Conference. The definition now reads:

Commissioning is the act of the church that publicly acknowledges God's call and the response, talents, gifts, and training of the candidate. The church invokes the Holy Spirit as the candidate is commissioned to be a faithful servant leader among the people, to lead the church in service, to proclaim the Word of God, and to equip others for ministry.

Through commissioning, the church sends persons in leadership and service in the name of Jesus Christ and marks their entrance into a time of probation as they prepare for ordination. Commissioned ministers are probationary clergy members of the annual conference and are accountable to the bishop and the clergy session for the conduct of their ministry.

During probation, the clergy session discerns their fitness for ordination and their effectiveness in ministry. After fulfilling all candidacy requirements, and upon recommendation of the conference board of ordained ministry, the clergy session shall vote on the probationary membership and commissioning of the candidates. The bishop and secretary of the conference shall provide credentials as a probationary member and a commissioned minister in the annual conference.

The period of commissioned ministry is concluded when the probationary members are: received as full members of the annual conference and ordained either deacon or elder; or a decision is made not to proceed toward ordination and probationary membership is ended.[1]

This change attempts to clarify the difference between ordination and commissioning by defining commissioning as an affirmation of the candidate and as a time of discernment by the conference. It is specifically related to probationary membership with a defined ending, and, therefore, does not carry the lifelong quality of ordination. It is clear that commissioning is the beginning of a process that culminates in ordination. The definition responds to many of the concerns raised in chapter 4 and, it is hoped, will assist the church as we seek to give meaning to this new liturgical creation.

B. Licensing

Two significant changes were made in relation to licensing of commissioned ministers. First, a commissioned minister preparing for ordination as a deacon will be licensed "for the practice of ministry during probationary membership to perform the duties of the ministry of the deacon" as stated in ¶ 319.[2] Though it is still not clear as to just what this license is, it is an important step in terms of authorization of commissioned ministers by the annual conference for the practice of ministry.

The second change addresses the confusion between licensed local pastors and the licensing of commissioned ministers preparing for ordination as elders who are serving as pastors. Under the 1996 legislation commissioned ministers were simply granted a local pastor license to authorize them for pastoral leadership. This created confusion as to individuals' status since they were both commissioned probationary members and licensed local pastors. In order to create a distinction between the two categories, ¶ 340 defines two categories of "licensing for pastoral ministry"—one for commissioned ministers and the other for local pastors.

These two changes, then, confirm the fact that commissioning does not authorize anyone for the practice of ministry; rather, it celebrates the calling of the candidate and marks the entrance into probation. It is the license that authorizes persons to function on behalf of the annual conference during probation for ordination as either a deacon or an elder.

C. Laity in the Laying on of Hands

The continuing question of the participation of laity in the laying on of hands was addressed in part by changes in ¶ 321.6 and ¶ 324. In the ordination of both deacons and elders, the paragraphs are now consistent and read:

"The bishop shall be assisted by other deacons (or elders) and may include laity designated by the bishop representing the

Church community and representatives of other Christian communions in the laying on of hands."[3]

It is now clear that deacons will assist in the ordination of deacons, and elders will assist in the ordination of elders, representing the Order into which the person is being ordained. Laity involved must be chosen by the bishop to represent the community rather than the personal choice of the ordinand. Though this is permissible (leaving the decision in the hands of the individual bishop), it will be difficult for any individual bishop to deny lay participation, and this practice will likely become the pattern for United Methodist ordination, a significant break from our Anglican roots and a move closer to the free-church tradition.

D. Changes That Were Not Approved

It is also important to note some of the proposed changes that were not approved by the General Conference:

1. A resolution calling for sacramental authority for the deacon was rejected by the legislative committee, thus affirming that the ministry of the deacon and the elder are meant to be distinct and that the sacramental ministry is to be part of the ministry of the elder.

2. Two proposals attempted to take us back to the pre-1996 ordering of ministry by calling for the reinstitution of (1) ordination as deacon prior to elders ordination, and (2) the consecration of diaconal ministers. Both were defeated by the legislative committee.

3. Several changes in the ordering of ministry were proposed earlier by the General Commission on Christian Unity and Interreligious Concerns in an attempt to make our legislation more accommodating to the reception of clergy from other denominations and to the ecumenical consensus. These proposals were withdrawn, based on the commitment of the Division of Ordained Ministry to call together consultations during the next quadrennium to discuss these matters in depth.

In short, the 2000 General Conference was not inclined to make any significant changes in the ordering of ministry. Substantially all the legislation coming from the Division was approved, and few of the proposals calling for major change were adopted. After more than two decades of heated debate about the orders of ministry, the 2000 General Conference chose not to debate it at all, except as it related to the larger question of homosexuality. This long-awaited hiatus creates a welcome space for reflective study and prayerful consideration of the direction of ordained ministry in The United Methodist Church under the leadership of the Division of Ordained Ministry and the Council of Bishops. As we seek God's leadership for the rapidly advancing future, may the same spirit that inspired the prophets and apostles, John Wesley and Francis Asbury, Philip Otterbein and Jacob Albright, empower us for effective witness on behalf of our Lord and Savior Jesus Christ.

Notes:

1. Unpublished first draft of ministry legislation (Nashville: General Board of Higher Education and Ministry, June 2000), ¶ 316, p. 18.
2. Ibid., ¶ 317.1, p. 19.
3. Ibid., ¶ 321.6, p. 24; ¶ 324.3, p. 28.

Notes

Introduction

1. *Perspectives in American Methodism: Interpretive Essays,* Russell E. Richey, Kenneth E. Rowe, and Jean Miller Schmidt, eds. (Nashville: Kingswood Books, 1993), 431-47.

2. Bishop William Cannon, "Meaning of Ministry in Methodism," *Methodist History* 8, no. 1 (October 1969), 3.

3. Franz Hildebrandt, "The Meaning of Ordination in Methodism," in *Ministry in The Methodist Heritage* (Nashville: Board of Higher Education, 1960), 67.

4. William B. Lawrence, "The Theology of Ordained Ministry in The United Methodist Church," *Quarterly Review* 18/1 (Spring 1998): 74. Used by permission.

5. Thomas E. Frank, *Polity, Practice, and Mission of The United Methodist Church* (Nashville: Abingdon Press, 1997), 149-50.

6. Ibid., 176.

7. Ibid., 179.

8. Unless another year is noted, all citations of the *Book of Discipline* and all paragraph numbers noted in parentheses within the text refer to *The Book of Discipline of The United Methodist Church—1996* (Nashville: The United Methodist Publishing House, 1996).

1. History and Identity

1. Bishop William Cannon, "Meaning of Ministry in Methodism," *Methodist History* 8, no. 1 (October 1969): 8.

2. It is important to note that the British Methodist Church and some of the other traditions that make up The United Methodist Church today did not follow this pattern of ordination.

3. Richard P. Heitzenrater, *Wesley and the People Called Methodist* (Nashville: Abingdon Press, 1995), 288.

4. A. Raymond George, "Ordination in Methodism," *London Quarterly and Holburn Review* (1951): 160.

5. Linda Durbin, "The Nature of Ordination in Wesley's View of the Ministry," *Methodist History* 9, no.3 (April 1971): 3.

6. "Large Minutes," *Works of John Wesley,* vol. 8, 3rd ed. (Grand Rapids: Baker Book House, 1978), 309.

7. See "Sermon CXV: The Ministerial Office." *Works of John Wesley,* vol. 7, 3rd ed. (Grand Rapids: Baker Book House, 1978), 273-81. In fact, during his ministry in Georgia Wesley refused to serve Communion to anyone who had not been baptized by a properly ordained Anglican priest.

8. Ibid., 7:11.

9. Wesley came to believe that the church can give a person authority to execute the office, but that prior to that there must be an inward call from God. E. Herbert Nygren concludes that Wesley was "convinced that no ordination is valid if the one being ordained has received no inward call from God. The consecration doesn't impart the Holy Ghost, for this gift does not trickle down through a set of hands but is poured out by God himself upon the spirit of the man." E. Herbert Nygren, "John Wesley's Changing Concept of Ministry," *Religion in Life* 31, no. 2 (Spring, 1962): 274.

10. David Shipley, "The Ministry in Methodism in the Eighteenth Century," *Ministry in the Methodist Heritage* (Nashville: Board of Higher Education, 1960), 16.

11. John Wesley, *Life of the Rev. John Wesley,* vol. 5, *Works of John Wesley on Compact Disc* (Nashville: Providence House Publishers, 1995), 541.

12. Ibid., 541.

13. Dennis Campbell, *The Yoke of Obedience* (Nashville: Abingdon Press, 1988), 62.

14. Durbin, "The Nature of Ordination," 13.

15. Cannon, "Meaning of Ministry," 11.

16. Heitzenrater, *Wesley,* 285.

17. Cannon, "Meaning of Ministry," 10.

18. "To 'Our Brethren in America,' 10 September, 1784," *Letters of John Wesley,* vol. 7, ed., John Telford (London: Epworth, 1931), 238-39.

19. John A. Eversole, "A Re-examination of American Methodist Ordination," *Iliff Review* 20, no. 3 (Fall 1963): 11.

20. Ibid., 11.

21. Russell Richey discusses these key events in *The Methodist Conference in America* (Nashville: Kingswood Books, 1996).

22. Though not directly related to our study of ordination, it is important to note that this conference also legislated against slavery. It required that Methodist preachers not hold slaves and that they preach against slavery. See Richey, *The Methodist Conference*, 28.

23. *History of American Methodism,* vol. 1, ed. Emory Stevens Bucke (Nashville: Abindgon Press, 1964), 210.

24. Wesley was horrified. He wrote to Asbury, September 17, 1788: "How can you, how dare you suffer yourself to be called bishop? I shudder, I start at the very thought! Men may call me a knave or a fool, a rascal, a scoundrel, and I am content; but they shall never by my consent call me bishop! For my sake, for God's sake, put a full end to this." *Letters,* 8:91.

25. David Steinmetz, *Memory and Mission* (Nashville: Abingdon Press, 1988), 83.

26. Ibid., 83.

27. *The Journal and Letters of Francis Asbury,* vol. 2, ed. Elmer T. Clark (Nashville: Abingdon Press, 1958), 469-70.

28. Steinmetz, *Memory,* 95.

29. Ibid., 93-94.

30. Ibid., 12.

31. Thomas E. Frank, *Polity, Practice, and Mission of The United Methodist Church* (Abingdon Press, 1997), 58.

32. Jeffrey P. Mickle, "A Comparison of the Doctrine of Ministry in Francis Asbury and Philip Otterbein," *Methodist History* 19, no. 4 (July 1981): 191.

33. Ibid., 187-205.

34. Ibid., 192.

35. Ibid., 192ff., for detailed discussion.

36. Ibid., 195.

37. Ibid., 195.

38. Ibid., 202-4.

39. Ibid., 205.

40. For a discussion of this trend, see Frank, *Polity.*

41. Richey, *Methodist Conference,* 70.

42. William B. Lawrence, "The Theology of Ordained Ministry in The United Methodist Church," *Quarterly Review* 18/1 (Spring 1998): 77.

43. Richey, *Methodist Conference,* 38-39.

44. Ibid., 226

45. Ibid., 87-88.

46. Ibid., 99.

47 Ibid., 95-108.

48. Ibid., 109.

49. Ibid., 89-90.

50. *The Doctrines and Discipline of the Methodist Church* (New York: The Methodist Book Concern, 1939), ¶ 223, pp. 68-69.

51. Ibid., ¶ 392, pp 114-15.

52. Richard P. Heitzenrater, "A Critical Analysis of the Ministry Studies Since 1944," in Russell E. Richey et al., *Perspectives on American Methodism: Interpretive Essays,* ed. Jean Miller Schmidt (Nashville: Abingdon Press, 1993).

53. Ibid., 435

54. Ibid., 435-36.

55. *The Book of Discipline of The United Methodist Church—1968* (Nashville: The Methodist Publishing House, 1968), ¶ 307.1-2, p. 108.

56. Ibid., ¶ 307.3.

57. Ibid., ¶ 501, p. 149-50.

58. Ibid., ¶ 504, p. 150.

59. Ibid., ¶ 308.2, p. 109.

2. Ordination Within the Ministry of All Christians

1. See Richard P. Heitzenrater's review of the series of ministry study proposals, "A Critical Analysis of the Ministry Studies Since 1944," in Russell E. Richey et al., *Perspectives on American Methodism: Interpretive Essays,* ed. Jean Miller Schmidt (Nashville: Abingdon Press, 1993).

2. World Council of Churches, *Baptism, Eucharist and Ministry,* Faith and Order Paper, no. 11 (Geneva: World Council of Churches, 1982), 20.

3. Bishop David Lawson, personal letter, July 13, 1998. Used by permission.

4. James Garlow, "The Layperson as Minister," in *The Church: An Inquiry into Ecclesiology,* ed. Melvin Deiter (Anderson, Ind.: Warner Press, 1984), 436.

5. "A Farther Appeal to Men and Religion," *The Works of John Wesley on Compact Disc,* vol. 3 (Nashville: Providence House Publishers, 1995), 220.

6. Ibid., 221.

7. Ibid., 222.

8. Harold Burgess, "A Wesleyan Theology of Ministry," *Wesleyan Theological Journal* 18, no. 1 (Spring 1983): 20.

9. Margaret Batty and Geoffrey Melburn, *Workaday Preachers* (Peterborough, England: Methodist Publishing House, 1995), 135.

10. Earl G. Hunt and Ezra Earl Jones, *Prophetic Evangelist* (Nashville: General Board of Discipleship, 1993), 18.

11. Ibid., 9.

12. Paul Chilcote, *John Wesley and the Women Preachers of Early Methodism* (Metuchen, N.J.: Scarecrow Press, 1991), 22.

13. Thomas E. Frank, *Polity, Practice, and Mission of The United Methodist Church* (Abingdon Press, 1997), 180.

14. Virginia Law, *Appointment Congo* (New York: Rand McNally, 1966), 71.

15. "National Plan for Hispanic Ministries: The Report to General Conference 2000," *Daily Christian Advocate Advance Edition,* vol. 1, sec. 2 (Nashville: The United Methodist Publishing House, 2000), 832.

16. Ibid., 832.

17. Howard Belben, *Ministry in the Local Church* (London: Epworth Press, 1986), 14.

18. James Fenhagen, *Ministry for a New Time* (Bethesda, Md.: Alban Institute, 1995), xii.

3. Toward New Understanding of Ordination

1. William B. Lawrence, "The Theology of Ordained Ministry in The United Methodist Church," *Quarterly Review* 18/1 (spring 1998): 83.

2. Ibid., 83.

3. Ibid., 82.

4. Dennis Campbell, *Who Will Go for Us?* (Nashville: Abingdon Press, 1994), 61.

5. David Bartlett, *Ministry in the New Testament* (Minneapolis: Fortress Press, 1994), 121.

6. Ibid., 122.

7. Frederick Buechner, *A Room Called Remember* (San Francisco: Harper & Row, 1984), 148.

8. General Board of Discipleship, *Services for the Ordering of Ministry in The United Methodist Church: Provisional Texts* (Nashville: The United Methodist Publishing House, 1998), 21.

9. For full discussion see Russell E. Richey, *The Methodist Conference in America: A History* (Nashville: Kingswood Books, 1996).

10. Ibid., 17.

11. General Board of Discipleship, *Services,* 25.

4. Commissioning and Ordaining

1. See the "The Study of the Ministry," a report of the Council of Bishops to the 1996 General Conference in the *Daily Christian Advocate Advance Edition* (Nashville: The United Methodist Publishing House, 1996) 1:978-79.

2. General Conference referred the revision of the ordinal to the Board of Discipleship in consultation with the Board of Higher Education and Ministry and the Council of Bishops. The result was the Ordinal Revision Working Group, from here on referred to as the working group.

3. General Board of Discipleship, *Services for the Ordering of Ministry in The United Methodist Church: Provisional Texts* (Nashville: The United Methodist Publishing House, 1998), 6. See appendix, p. 155.

4. Ibid., 7. See appendix, 156.

5. Ibid., 7-8. See appendix, 157.

6. Ibid., 49-51.

7. Ibid., see appendix, 157.

8. Mary Elizabeth Moore, response to the working group, November 1997.

9. General Board of Discipleship *Services,* 8. See appendix, 158.

10. Ibid., 9. See appendix, 160.

11. Quoted in David Tripp's "Ordination, Laying on of Hands, and The Role of The Laity," *Doxology* (December 1998), 42.

12. Ibid., 53.

13. Ibid., 54.

14. Ibid., 54.

15. General Board of Discipleship, *Services,* 9. See appendix, 161.

16. Ibid., 10. See appendix, 161.

17. Ibid., 49 (see 52ff. for the text of this service).

5. Servant Ministry, Representative Ministry, and Apostolic Ministry

1. Richard P. Heitzenrater, "A Critical Analysis of the Ministry Studies Since 1944," in Russell E. Richey et al., *Perspectives on American Methodism,* ed. Jean Miller Schmidt (Nashville: Abingdon Press, 1993), 437.

2. William B. Lawrence, "The Theology of Ordained Ministry in The United Methodist Church," *Quarterly Review* 18/1 (Spring 1998): 80.

3. *Baptism, Eucharist and Ministry* uses the term "representative" in several places. It reads: "As heralds and ambassadors, ordained ministers are representatives of Jesus Christ to the community, and proclaim his message of reconciliation. . . . Any member of the Body may share in proclaiming and teaching the Word of God, may contribute to the sacramental life of that Body. The ordained ministry fulfills these functions in a representative way, providing the focus for the unity of the life and witness of the community." See World Council of Churches, *Baptism, Eucharist and Ministry,* Faith and Order Paper, no. 11 (Geneva: World Council of Churches, 1982), 21.

4. Richard P. Heitzenrater, "Critical Analysis," 440.

5. Thomas E. Frank, *Polity, Practice, and Mission of The United Methodist Church* (Nashville: Abingdon Press, 1997), 149-50.

6. Ibid., 149-50.

7. Lawrence, "Theology," 81.

8. Robert Neville, "The Apostolic Character of Ordained Ministry," *Quarterly Review* 10, no. 4 (Winter 1990).

9. Ibid., 5.

10. Ibid., 7-8.

11. Ibid., 13.

6. The Traveling Elder in Full Connection

1. Compare ¶¶ 116, 303.2, and 310 in the 1996 *Book of Discipline.*

2. See David Steinmetz's discussion of Word and Sacrament in *Memory and Mission* (Abingdon Press, 1988), 70.

3. World Council of Churches, *Baptism, Eucharist and Ministry,* Faith and Order Paper no. 11 (Geneva: World Council of Churches, 1982), 22.

4. Steinmetz, *Memory and Mission,* 70.

5. Thomas E. Frank, *Polity, Practice, and Mission of The United Methodist Church* (Nashville: Abingdon Press, 1997), 42.

6. World Council of Churches, *Baptism, Eucharist and Ministry,* 27.

7. Dennis Campbell, *Who Will Go for Us?* (Nashville: Abingdon Press, 1994), 68, 106.

8. Frank, *Polity,* p. 42-43.

9. Richard P. Heitzenrater, "A Critical Analysis of the Ministry Studies Since 1944," *Occasional Paper No. 76* (Nashville: United Methodist Board of Higher Education and Ministry, September 1988), 4.

10. Abel Stevens, *An Essay on Church Polity* (New York: Lance and Tippett, 1848), 187.

7. Ordaining a New Deacon

1. Kenneth E. Rowe, "The Ministry of the Deacons in Methodism from Wesley to Today," a paper presented to the Northeast Jurisdiction Conference on Effectiveness in Ministry, Hershey, Penn., 1998, p. 1.

2. Ben L. Hartley and Paul Van Buren, *The Deacon: Ministry Through Words of Faith and Acts of Love* (Nashville: General Board of Higher Education and Ministry, 1999), 4.

3. Robin Lovin, "Critical Issues for the Ordering of Ministry and the Ordination of Ministers," report to the United Methodist Ordinal Task Force, December 1997, p. 1.

4. Ibid., 2.

5. Since *diaconia* means both ministry and service, the words are interchangeable and speak to the ministry of the whole church, the body of Christ. Though the ministry of the deacon may focus on service, *diaconia*/service/ministry is not limited to the deacon.

6. See chapter 3, "Ordination Within the Ministry of All Christians."

7. See chapter 3 and the suggestion for future understandings of ordination.

8 Hartley and Van Buren, *The Deacon,* 54, 57.

9. Lovin, "Critical Issues," 4.

10. See James Barnett, *The Diaconate: A Full and Equal Order* (Valley Forge: Trinity Press International, 1985), for a detailed history of the diaconate.

11. Daniel Benedict and Anne Burnette Hook, *Worship Matters: A United Methodist Guide to Ways to Worship,* vol. 1, ed. E. Byron Anderson (Nashville: Discipleship Resources, 1999), 134.

12. Ibid., 135.

13. Ibid., 130.

14. Hartley and Van Buren, *The Deacon,* p. 60.

8. The Evolution of the Local Preacher to Local Pastor

1. Frederick Norwood, "The Americanization of the Wesleyan Itinerant," in *Ministry in the Methodist Heritage* (Nashville: Board of Higher Education and Ministry, 1960), 34.

2. Ibid., 34.

3. Frederick Norwood, "The Shaping of Methodist Ministry," *Religion in Life* 42, no. 3 (Autumn 1974): 340.

4. Norwood, "The Americanization of the Wesleyan Itinerant," 45.

5. From the 1798 *Book of Discipline,* quoted in "Itinerate and Local Elders in the United Methodist Church," by Robert F. Kohler and Ann B. Sherer in a paper presented to the Council of Bishops' Ministry Study Committee, Nashville, Tenn., December 4, 1994, p. 1.

6. Ibid., 2.

7. Norwood, "The Shaping of Methodist Ministry," 339.

8. *The Doctrines and Discipline of the Methodist Episcopal Church, South* (Publishing House Methodist Church, South, 1926), ¶ 139, p. 77.

9. *Doctrines and Disciplines of the Methodist Church* (New York: The Methodist Book Concern, 1939), ¶ 287, p. 88.

10. See *The Book of Discipline of the United Methodist Church—1992* (Nashville: The United Methodist Publishing House, 1992), ¶ 419, p. 220.

11. Dennis Campbell, *The Yoke of Obedience* (Nashville: Abingdon Press), 79.

9. Conference Membership, Itineracy, and Ordination

1. Thomas E. Frank, *Polity, Practice, and Mission of the United Methodist Church* (Nashville: Abingdon Press, 1997), 175.

2. Ibid., 176.

3. Ibid., 176.

4. Ibid., 177.

5. Russell Richey, *Connectionalism: Ecclesiology, Mission and Identity, United Methodism and American Culture,* vol. 1 (Nashville: Abingdon Press, 1997), 4.

6. William Oden, "Without Reserve: A Critical Appreciation of Itineracy," in *Send Me? The Itineracy in Crisis,* ed. Donald Messer (Nashville: Abingdon Press, 1991), 57.

7. *Doctrines and Discipline of the Methodist Church* (New York: The Methodist Book Concern, 1939), ¶ 212.5, p. 64.

8. Oden, "Without Reserve," 51.

9. Donald Treese, "Reaffirming the Covenant in Itineracy," in *Send Me?* 75.

10. Frank, *Polity,* 195.

11. Richey, *Connectionalism,* 4-6.

12. Frank, *Polity,* p. 178.

13. Richey, *Connectionalism,* 5.

14. Frank, *Polity,* 155.

15. Treese, "Reaffirming," 72.

16. Ibid., 73.

17. Ibid., 73.

18. See Russell Richey, *The Methodist Conference in America: A History* (Nashville: Kingswood Books, 1996), 22ff., for a detailed discussion of the nature and purpose of the early conferences.

10. Summary

1. See Richard P. Heitzenrater, "A Critical Analysis of Ministry Studies Since 1944," in Russell E. Richey et al., *Perspectives on American Methodism: Interpretive Essays,* ed. Jean Miller Schmidt (Nashville: Abingdon Press, 1993) 431-37. Frederick A. Norwood, "The Shaping of Methodist Ministry," *Religion in Life* 43, no. 3 (Autumn 1974): 337; and Kenneth E. Rowe, "The Ministry of Deacons in Methodism from Wesley to Today," a paper presented to the Northeast Jurisdiction Conference on Effectiveness in Ministry, Hershey, Penn. (February 2-4, 1998), among others.

2. Dennis Campbell, *The Yoke of Obedience* (Nashville: Abingdon Press, 1988), 52.

3. Ibid., 80-81.

4. *The Methodist Hymnal* (Nashville: Board of Publication of the United Methodist Church, 1964), no. 829.

5. Ibid., no. 464.

6. Charles Wesley, "A Charge to Keep I Have," *The United Methodist Hymnal* (Nashville: The United Methodist Publishing House, 1989), no. 413.

Selected Bibliography

Asbury, Francis. *The Journal and Letters of Francis Asbury.* Vol. 2. Edited by Elmer T. Clark. Nashville: Abingdon Press, 1958.

Baker, Frank. *From Wesley to Asbury: Studies in Early American Methodism.* Durham: Duke University Press, 1976.

Bangs, Nathan. *Vindication of Methodist Episcopacy.* Published by Nathan Bangs, Methodist Episcopal Church, New York, 1820.

Barnett, James Monroe. *The Diaconate: A Full and Equal Order.* Valley Forge: Trinity Press International, 1985.

Bartlett, David. *Ministry in the New Testament.* Minneapolis: Fortress Press, 1993.

Batty, Margaret and Geoffrey Melburn. *Workaday Preachers.* Peterborough, England: Methodist Publishing House, 1995.

Belben, Howard. *Ministry in the Local Church.* London: Epworth Press, 1986.

The Book of Discipline of The United Methodist Church—1968. Nashville: Methodist Publishing House, 1968.

The Book of Discipline of The United Methodist Church—1992. Nashville: The United Methodist Publishing House, 1992.

The Book of Discipline of The United Methodist Church—1996. Nashville: The United Methodist Publishing House, 1996.

Buechner, Frederick. *A Room Called Remember.* San Francisco: Harper & Row, 1984.

Burgess, Harold. "A Wesleyan Theology of Ministry." *Wesleyan Theological Journal* 18, no. 1 (Spring 1983): 20.

Campbell, Dennis. *The Yoke of Obedience.* Nashville: Abingdon Press, 1988.

_____. *Who Will Go for Us?* Nashville: Abingdon Press, 1994.

Cannon, Bishop William. "The Meaning of Ministry in Methodism," *Methodist History* 8, no.1 (October 1969): 3-19.

_____. "Holy Spirit in Vatican II and in the Writings of Wesley." *Religion in Life* 37, no. 3 (Autumn 1968): 440.

Carroll, Jackson W. *As One with Authority: Reflective Leadership in Ministry.* Louisville: Westminster/John Knox Press, 1991.

Chapman, David. "Koinonia and Ordination." *Epworth Review* 23 (Spring 1996): 76-83.

Chilcote, Paul. *John Wesley and the Women Preachers of Early Methodism.* Metuchen, N.J.: Scarecrow Press, 1991.

The Church: An Inquiry into Ecclesiology. Edited by Daniel Berg and Melvin Dieter. Anderson, Ind.: Warner Press, 1984.

Conklin, Faith. "To Serve the Present Age: Reflections on the Ministry Study Report." *Quarterly Review* 8, no. 1 (Spring 1988): 30.

Connectionalism: Ecclesiology, Mission and Identity. Vol. 1 of *United Methodism and American Culture.* Edited by Dennis Campbell, William Lawrence, and Russell Richey. Nashville: Abingdon Press, 1997.

Dahlstrom, Earl C. "For the Building of the Church." *Covenant Quarterly* 338 (May 1980): 3-8

Dawes, Stephen. "Ordination in the Methodist Church—An Outdated Practice?" *Epworth Review* 18 (Spring 1991): 22-25.

Discipleship Resources. *Worship Matters: A United Methodist Guide to Ways to Worship.* Edited by E. Bryon Anderson. Nashville: Discipleship Resources, 1999.

Doctrines and Disciplines of the Methodist Episcopal Church, South. Nashville: Publishing House Methodist Episcopal Church, South, 1926.

Doctrines and Disciplines of the Methodist Church. New York: The Methodist Book Concern, 1939.

Durbin, Linda. "The Nature of Ordination in Wesley's View of the Ministry." *Methodist History* 8 (April 1971): 3-20.

Eversole, John A. "Re-examination of American Methodist Ordination." *Iliff Review* 20, no. 3 (Fall 1963): 11.

Fenhagen, James. *Ministry for a New Time*. Bethesda, Md.: Alban Institute, 1995.

Frank, Thomas. *Polity, Practice and Mission of The United Methodist Church*. Nashville: Abingdon Press, 1997.

Garlow, James. *John Wesley's Understanding of the Laity as Demonstrated by His Use of the Lay Preachers*. Doctoral Thesis, Drew University, 1979.

____. "The Layperson as Minister," in *The Church: An Inquiry Into Ecclesiology*. Edited by Melvin Deiter. Anderson, Ind.: Warner Press, 1984.

General Board of Discipleship. *Services for the Ordering of Ministry in The United Methodist Church: Provisional Texts*. Nashville: The United Methodist Publishing House, 1998.

George, Raymond A. "Ordination in Methodism." *London Quarterly and Holburn Review* (1951): 160.

Gerdes, Egon W. *Informed Ministry: Theological Reflections of the Practice of Ministry in Methodism*. Zurich: Publishing House of The United Methodist Church, 1976.

Harkness, Georgia. *The Church and Its Laity*. Nashville: Abingdon Press, 1962.

Hartley, Ben L. "Resource Book for the Work of the Deacon." A manuscript. Nashville: General Board of Higher Education and Ministry, 1998.

Hartley, Ben L. and Paul Van Buren. *The Deacon: Words of Faith and Acts of Love*. Nashville: General Board of Higher Education and Ministry, 1999.

Heitzenrater, Richard P. "A Critical Analysis of Ministry Studies Since 1944." *Perspectives on American Methodism: Interpretive Essays*. Russell Richey et al. Edited by Jean Miller Schmidt. Nashville: Abingdon Press, 1993, 431-47.

____. "A Critical Analysis of Ministry Studies Since 1944." *Occasional Paper,* no. 76. Nashville: General Board of Higher Education and Ministry, September 1988.

____. *Wesley and the People Called Methodist*. Nashville: Abingdon Press, 1995.

Hildebrandt, Franz. "The Meaning of Ordination in Methodism." *Ministry in The Methodist Heritage*. Nashville: Board of Higher Education, 1960: 67.

The History of American Methodism, 3 vols. Edited by Emory Stevens Bucke. Nashville: Abingdon Press, 1964.

Holter, Donald W. "Some Changes Related to the Ordained Ministry in the History of American Methodism." *Methodist History* 13, no. 3 (April 1975): 177-94.

____. "The Future of the Diaconate: Christian Unity Group." *One in Christ: A Catholic Ecumenical Journal* 18, no. 1 (1982): 60.

"Itineracy in The United Methodist Church Today: A Roundtable." Edited by Sharon Hels. *Quarterly Review* 11 (Summer 1991): 449.

Keller, Rosemary Skinner, Gerald F. Moede, and Mary Elizabeth Moore. "Called to Serve: The United Methodist Diaconate." Nashville: General Board of Higher Education and Ministry, 1987.

Kelley, Alden D. *The People of God: A Study of the Doctrine of the Laity.* Connecticut: Seabury Press, 1962.

Kohler, Robert F. and Ann B. Sherer, "Itinerate and Local Elders in The United Methodist Church." A paper presented to the Council of Bishops Ministry Study Committee, Nashville, Tenn. (December 4, 1994).

Kriewald, Diedra. "Ministerial Formation: Laos and Diaconia" A paper presented to the Northeast Jurisdiction Conference on Effectiveness in Ministry, Hershey, Penn. (February 1998).

Law, Virginia. *Appointment Congo.* New York: Rand McNally, 1966.

Lawrence, William B. "The Theology of Ordained Ministry in The United Methodist Church." *Quarterly Review* 18, no.1 (Spring 1998): 71-87.

Lawson, Bishop David. Letter to author, July 13, 1998.

Lovin, Robin. "Critical Issues for the Ordering of Ministry and the Ordination of Ministers." A report to the United Methodist Ordinal Task Force. Nashville, December 1997.

McNeal, Reggie. *Revolution in Leadership.* Nashville: Abingdon Press, 1998.

The Methodist Hymnal, 1964. Nashville: The Methodist Publishing House, 1964.

Mickle, Jeffrey. "Comparison of the Doctrines of Ministry of Francis Asbury and Phillip Otterbein." *Methodist History* 19, no. 4, (July 1981): 187.

Moss, Arthur Bruce. "The Ordination of Frances Asbury (T. C. Ruckle's Painting)." *Methodist History* 1 (April 1963): 25-28.

Mott, John R. "Liberating the Lay Forces of Christianity: The Ayre Lectures of 1931." *Colgate Rochester Divinity School Journal.* New York: MacMillan, 1932.

Neville, Robert. "The Apostolic Character of Ordained Ministry." *Quarterly Review* 10 (Winter 1990): 4.

Norwood, Frederick. "The Shaping of Methodist Ministry." *Religion in Life* 43, no. 3 (Autumn 1974): 337.

____. "The Americanization of the Wesleyan Itinerant." *Ministry in The Methodist Heritage.* Nashville: Board of Higher Education and Ministry, 1960.

Nygren, E. Herbert. "John Wesley's Changing Concept of Ministry." *Religion in Life* 31, (Spring 1962): 266.

Oden, Bishop William. "Without Reserve: A Critical Appreciation of Itineracy." *Send Me? The Itineracy in Crisis.* Edited by Donald Messer. Nashville: Abingdon Press, 1991.

The People(s) Called Methodist: Forms and Reforms of Their Life. Vol. 2 of *United Methodism and American Culture.* Edited by Dennis Campbell, William Lawrence, and Russell E. Richey. Nashville: Abingdon Press, 1997.

Perspectives on American Methodism: Interpretive Essays. Edited by Russell E. Richey, Kenneth Rowe, and Jean Miller Schmidt. Nashville: Abingdon Press, 1993.

Prophetic Evangelist: The Living Legacy of Harry Denman. Edited by Bishop Earl G. Hunt and Ezra Earl Jones. Nashville: General Board of Discipleship, 1993.

Richey, Russell. "Evolving Patterns of Methodist Ministry." *Methodist History.* Vol. 22 (October 1983).

____. *The Methodist Conference in America: A History.* Nashville: Kingswood Books, 1996.

Rowe, Kenneth. "The Ministry of Deacons in Methodism from Wesley to

Today (1998)." A paper presented to the Northeast Jurisdiction Conference on Effectiveness in Ministry. Hershey, Penn., February 24, 1998.

Runyon, Ted. *The New Creation: John Wesley's Theology Today.* Nashville: Abingdon Press, 1998.

Sanders, Paul. "An Appraisal of John Wesley's Sacramentalism in the Evolution of Early American Methodism." Ph.D. diss., Union Theological Seminary, 1954.

Send Me? The Itineracy in Crisis. Edited by Donald Messer. Nashville: Abingdon Press, 1991.

Shipley, David. "The Ministry in Methodism in the Eighteenth Century." In *Ministry in the Methodist Heritage.* Edited by Gerald O. McCulloh. Nashville: The Methodist Church, Board of Education, 1960.

Spellmann, Norman Woods. "The General Superintendency in American Methodism, 1784-1870." Ph.D. diss., Yale University, April 1961.

Steinmetz, David C. "Asbury's Doctrine of Ministry." *Duke Divinity School Review* 40 (Winter 1975): 10-17.

_____. *Memory and Mission.* Nashville: Abingdon Press,1988.

Stevens, Abel. "An Essay on Church Polity." New York: Lance and Tippett, 1848.

Treese, Donald. "Reaffirming the Covenant in Itineracy." *Send Me? The Itineracy in Crisis.* Edited by Donald Messer. Nashville: Abingdon Press, 1991.

Tripp, David. "Ordination, Laying on of Hands and the Role of the Laity." *Doxology* (December 1998): 42-54.

The United Methodist Hymnal. Nashville: The United Methodist Publishing House, 1989.

Wesley, John. "Address to the Clergy." *Works of John Wesley.* Vol. 10. London: Wesleyan Conference Office, 1872. 480-506.

_____. "A Farther Appeal to Men and Religion." *Works of John Wesley on Compact Dsic.* Vol. 3. Nashville: Providence House Publishers, 1995.

_____. "Sermon CXV: The Ministerial Office." *Works of John Wesley.* Vol. 7, 3rd ed. Grand Rapids: Baker Book House, 1978.

_____. "Large Minutes, Role of the Helper." *Works of John Wesley.* Vol. 7, 3rd ed. Grand Rapids: Baker Book House, 1978. 309-21.

_____. *John Wesley's Sunday Services of the Methodists in North America.* Methodist Bicentennial Commemorative Reprint. Nashville: Methodist Publishing House, 1984.

_____. *Journal of the Rev. John Wesley.* Edited by Nehemiah Curnock. London: Charles Kelly Publishers, 1909.

_____. *Works of John Wesley on Compact Disc.* Providence House Publishers, Franklin, Tenn., 1995.

Wesleyan Theology: A Sourcebook. Edited by Thomas Langford. Durham: Labyrinth Press, 1984.

World Council of Churches. *Baptism, Eucharist and Ministry.* Faith and Order Paper No. 11. Geneva: World Council of Churches, 1982.

_____. *Churches Respond to Baptism, Eucharist and Ministry.* Vol. 2. Faith and Order Paper 132. Edited by Max Thurian. Geneva: World Council of Churches, 1986. 177.